Burning Beds
and
Mermaids

Stories for Advanced Listening and Conversation

Gail Feinstein Forman
San Diego Community College District

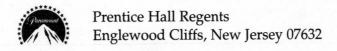
Prentice Hall Regents
Englewood Cliffs, New Jersey 07632

Library of Congress Cataloging-in-Publication Data

Forman, Gail Feinstein.
  Burning beds & mermaids / Gail Feinstein Forman.
      p.   cm.
  ISBN 0-13-101189--8
  1. English language -- Textbooks for foreign speakers.   2. Fulghum,
Robert--Adaptations.   3. Readers.   I.   Title. II.   Title: Burning
beds and mermaids.
PE1128.F583   1994
428.2'4--dc20   93-46207
                                        CIP

Acquistions Editor: Nancy Leonhardt
Production Editor: Janet Johnston
Director of Production and Manufacturing: David Riccardi
Editorial Production/Design Manager: Dominick Mosco
Production Coordinator: Ray Keating
Illustrator: Maxine Ann Sorokin
Cover Coordinator: Merle Krumper
Cover Designer: Rosemarie Paccione

Permission to reproduce audio excerpts from *All I Need to Know I Learned in Kindergarten* and
It Was On Fire When I Lay Down On It granted by Random House Audio Publishing Inc.

Permission to reproduce printed excerpts from *All I Need to Know I Learned in Kindergarten* and
It Was On Fire When I Lay Down On It granted by Villard Books, a division of Random House, Inc.

© 1994 by PRENTICE HALL REGENTS
Prentice-Hall, Inc.
A Paramount Communications Company
Englewood Cliffs, New Jersey 07632

Printed in the United States of America

10   9   8   7   6   5   4   3   2   1

ISBN 0-13-101189-8

Prentice-Hall International (UK) Limited, *London*
Prentice-Hall of Australia Pty. Limited, *Sydney*
Prentice-Hall Canada Inc., *Toronto*
Prentice-Hall Hispanoamericana, S.A., *Mexico*
Prentice-Hall of India Private Limited, *New Delhi*
Prentice-Hall of Japan, Inc., *Tokyo*
Simon & Schuster Asia Pte. Ltd., *Singapore*
Editora Prentice-Hall do Brasil, Ltda., *Rio de Janeiro*

Dedication

To my grandparents,
for braving the seas by ship
to this "Goldina Medina" (Golden Land).

To my parents,
for steering my ship on course.

To Yaakov,
for keeping my ship afloat.

CONTENTS

PREFACE

Mai, a bright but reticent Chinese student, came up to talk to me after our English class had finished.

Mai:	"Teacher, can I ask you a question?"
Teacher:	"Sure. What is it?"
Mai:	"Well, I want to ask you if the idiom we studied today, 'going from the frying pan into the fire,' has a meaning similar to 'It was on fire when I lay down on it.'"

At first I was taken aback by her astute observation. I was also surprised at her unusually bold behavior of approaching me face-to-face. She had sat in my class an entire semester, and this was the first time she had ever asked me a question!

Teacher:	"I'm surprised you remember the idiom about the burning bed! We studied it five months ago."
Mai:	"Oh yes, teacher. I loved the story. It was real life."

A few weeks before that, a similarly quiet, elderly Vietnamese student, who had arrived in class early, was feverishly writing, then checking another paper, then writing again.

Teacher:	"Hanh, it looks like you're working on a big project."
Hanh:	"Yes, teacher. I've almost finished. Almost."

Respecting my student's privacy, I decided not to ask any more about this "project." Instead I surreptitiously looked at the paper she was checking and saw that it was Fulghum's title essay from his *All I Really Need to Know I Learned in Kindergarten*, which I had used in class two months before. She was translating it from English to Vietnamese!

And so it went. Every once in a while, a student would make reference to a word or idea contained in the Fulghum essays that I had used in class the previous semester. After teaching ESL for ten years, I seemed to have finally hit upon some study material with magical universal appeal; students from many cultures in my class not only related to the essays but remembered their contents and learned from them. I wanted to make Fulghum's essays available and accessible to an even larger audience of English language students. I promised myself that I'd get back to this "someday" and develop the material further. This book is the result of that promise.

This promise could never have been fulfilled without the help and support of many giving people. First and foremost, I must offer giant-size balloons of gratitude to Robert Fulghum, who sustained my belief in miracles through our telephone conversations and through his successful efforts at Divine intervention. Ten thousand thank you's!!

For professional encouragement, I must thank Leann Howard for scribbling "Go for it" on all my teaching and program proposals. Thank you's also go to Gretchen Bitterlin for always taking the time to advise on class and program activities, and to Roberta Alexander for offering me the most recent floor for teaching exploration. An additional note of thanks to Robert Walsh for starting and encouraging me "on the road" to ESL. Also, I must include a thank you to Linda Sheldon at Random House for finding a way to make this book happen. For the actual production of this book, I must thank many at Prentice Hall—Nancy Leonhardt and Terry TenBarge for patience and advice throughout this circuitous process, Janet Johnston for excellent editorial advice, and Ken Clinton and Tom Dare for patiently and consistently following through on their marketing suggestions. Thanks also to Gene Garone at Pencil Point Studio for making the artistic vision come true.

Friendship of a special few has helped guide this particular being along myriad paths. Margo N. Tighe, tea-drinker extraordinaire, shared her thousand-cup teapot at every step along the continuum and picked me up from her floor when the occasion arose. A "Toda raba" to Annette Segal, the quintessential model and shaper of the phrase "Do it!," who shared with me the joys and discovery of the limitless possibilities within us and led me into the twentieth century with the Mac and a telephone-answering machine. Thanks to Maxine Sorokin, the book's illustrator and my good friend, whose conversations and pictures inspired me. Also in the friendship category, special thanks to Dr. Sheldon Hendler for his perception and direction to break through circles. And to Burt, Ellen, and Jeanne Bialik, for years of valued friendship and for presenting us with our first copy of It Was on Fire When I Lay Down on It. And to former student and friend Phu Luong, for providing me with a continuous example of insight and courage and for generously teaching and sharing the ways of T'ai Chi.

My family played a major role in getting me to this place in life. Special thanks to my mother and father, who I think knew this book might come about one day. To my grandfather "Pop," who left us the legacy of how to "make the best." To my cousin Judi Cooper, for cartwheels and support over many, many moons! To all my aunts and uncles, and especially to Bill and Kay Boyd, for their encouragement and assistance in both our California and New Jersey life. To my brother Mark and his wife,

Jo Anne, for helping us make a permanent home in California.

And to my husband, Jack, who equally shared in the birth of this book, for his flexibility, humor, and understanding over our twenty-two years together.

Anna, in the The King and I, aptly states that "when you become a teacher, by your students you'll be taught." To every student who walked through the doors of my classroom, for sharing your stories and yourself, **Thank you.**

TO THE TEACHER: SUGGESTIONS FOR USING THE TEXT

What Is *Burning Beds and Mermaids*?

Burning Beds and Mermaids is a unique ESL audio tape–text program. It is one book in a two-book ESL series based on best-selling author Robert Fulghum's books *All I Need to Know I Learned in Kindergarten* and *It Was on Fire When I Lay Down on It*. It is designed for intermediate to advanced students seeking engaging and challenging materials to strengthen communicative English language skills, particularly listening and conversation. The program is appropriate for both ESL and bilingual interactive skill courses in high school and for college credit ESL courses and non-credit adult education.

The book consists of ten chapters, each centered around a universal theme contained in one Fulghum essay. A variety of communicative exercises are provided on each essay's topics that are relevant to students' own experiences. Much emphasis is placed on cross-cultural issues, which are examined in several sections throughout each chapter. Conversations and situations used as examples in the book are based on actual classroom experiences. In addition, students are asked to practice language techniques in major academic skill areas, such as determining vocabulary meanings from context, reporting information, and preparing written and oral reports.

Why an ESL Text with a Listening Focus?

Research into the methods of second-language acquisition demonstrates that although listening is the most frequently used language skill, it is often given far too little emphasis in many ESL classrooms. Listening skills need to be seen as an active, not passive, skill area and should be part of the curriculum in order to improve students' comprehensive language understanding inside and outside the classroom.

This text-and-tape program was designed to develop ESL students' listening comprehension skills by using the basic principles of "focused listening." In focused listening exercises, students are asked to find specific information about something contained in a specific passage. Students demonstrate their comprehension by answering questions about that passage. They practice listening for a specific purpose by training themselves to focus only on the content necessary to meet that goal.

How to Use This Book and Audio Tape Program

Chapters are self-contained and therefore can be taught in any order. It is recommended, however, that the first and second chapters be taught first because each contains detailed instructions for using each chapter section in the succeeding chapters. Chapters 1 and 2 contain the introductory sections on determining vocabulary meaning from context. Teaching these chapters first will help both students and instructors become familiar with the format and goals of succeeding chapters.

Each chapter consists of five sections, each of which contains separate teaching instructions for that segment. Additional suggestions for methodology are provided in the following outline of chapter divisions.

1. Preview Section

Each chapter opens with an illustration page and a quotation related to the chapter theme. The illustrations are designed to be open-ended and sometimes have more than one possible interpretation. This open-endedness is intended to challenge students' imaginations and stimulate class discussion. The page following the illustration offers a brief text further developing the chapter theme.

Partner interviews follow, with exercises that reinforce the language of the student responses. Teachers are encouraged to use these **Preview** exercises as warm-ups for the actual essay and exercises that follow. In addition, the Preview exercises can be used to reinforce particular sentence structures or grammar being practiced in class at that time.

2. Vocabulary in Context and Quick-Check Sections

The exercises in this section introduce the key vocabulary words and phrases that students will hear in the audio essay. Chapters 1 and 2 introduce students to a series of reading techniques to assist them in finding out the meanings of unfamiliar vocabulary. The students are asked to use these techniques to figure out the meanings of words they don't understand. **Vocabulary definitions are given according to their usage in each specific essay.** A **Vocabulary Quick-Check** matching exercise follows to test students' comprehension of the new vocabulary.

3. Essay Preview Section

This section contains a brief introduction to the essay contents. It can be used as an additional warm-up and refocusing exercise for the essay to come.

4. Focused Listening Exercises

Students are provided many opportunities to be actively engaged in listening comprehension activities. Each **Focused Listening** section is divided into three sections:

Part One: Students demonstrate comprehension of the main content and details of the audio essay by answering the multiple choice questions. The audio essay is divided into segments and includes a brief narration and pause marking each individual section. Instructors may check student responses after each section, if desired.

Part Two: Students further demonstrate comprehension of the audio essay details by changing incorrect statements about the essay to correct statements. The essay is heard straight through, with no pauses or narration.

Dictation: Students listen to a segment of the tape for dictation practice and fill in the missing words.

Note: The complete text of each essay appears in the back of this book, and it can be useful for content or vocabulary review. It is advised, however, that students refer to the written text only after the listening exercises have been completed.

5. Class Activities Section

In these interactive skill exercises, students can work individually, in pairs, or in groups. Exercises in this section lay the foundation for more in-depth discussion of issues raised throughout each essay, and they can encourage use of additional materials related to these issues. The universality of the themes makes them suitable for a wide variety of realia.

The **Class Activity** sections are divided into three parts:

What Do You Think? Students answer questions about the essay orally or on paper. These questions are formulated to develop cross-cultural connections with the main ideas of the essay theme.

Reflections: This section provides readings and ideas for additional cross-cultural comparisons on theme-related issues.

Language of Culture: This unique section explores a significant communicative language strategy by using examples that appear in the essay. Situations and conversations are based on actual classroom experiences. The section offers opportunities to explore various cultural viewpoints and provides insight into various aspects of American culture.

Why Use Robert Fulghum's Material in ESL Classrooms?

The books of Robert Fulghum—minister, teacher, fiddler, and artist—have reached an extraordinarily large and diverse international audience. His books have topped best-seller lists for five years in a row and have been translated into more than twenty languages.

The main reasons Fulghum's essays are ideal source materials for ESL programs are the same reasons these books have achieved widespread recognition.

First, Fulghum's themes are truly universal. The everyman tales of his successes and failures cut across all cultural boundaries and can be understood by everyone. These short "slices of life" reflect the author's obsession with what he calls "exploring the meaning *in* life rather than *of* life." The stories are related with a unique blend of humor, honesty, and pathos; it is not surprising that many people are so easily drawn to Fulghum's writings. The universality of the themes—such as love, friendship, and personal dreams—will keep these stories fresh for many years, and this universality will expose ESL students to the ideas and expressive writing style of one of America's most popular writers.

Another reason the essays are well suited as ESL material is that their colorful, everyday language can be understood easily by non-native speakers. In addition, Fulghum's personal reading style on the audio tapes is unusually clear and engaging. He creates an instant bond with his audience, and each listener feels as if Fulghum were talking directly to him or her. Students are pulled into the narratives immediately, often feeling that they too have shared the experience. The stories become immediate "hooks," motivating students to concentrate on content as well as form—essential skills for the development of listening comprehension.

Finally, Fulghum's short essays are almost certain to have a personal impact on ESL students. The essays selected for this book are about remarkable, inspiring people and events. No matter what difficulties Fulghum's characters face, each essay always contains hope and optimism—or a life lesson to take home.

I have tried to provide class activities that stimulate the creative juices of both students and teachers. Feel free to adapt any of the suggested ideas to your own style—or create your own ideas. Because of my personal and classroom experience with Fulghum's essays, I feel confident that they will have a lasting impression on your class and on you.

Have fun!

Chapter 1

IT WAS ON FIRE WHEN I LAY DOWN ON IT

Sometimes we hear or read about a very unusual story. Often that story keeps coming back to our minds and remains an important memory.

With another student, look carefully at the picture on this page, which is about the story in the first chapter.

- What do you think the story is about?
- Do you think it might be about something unusual and unforgettable?
- In what ways do you think the chapter title and the quotation above the picture are related to the story?
- What do you think the burning bed means?

Share your ideas with your partner.

About Stories

Stories and storytellers are an important part of human history. Stories passed on from generation to generation preserve the traditions, beliefs, and customs of nations, cultures, and individuals. People around the world share a universal fascination with the reasons why things are the way they are, as well as a great curiosity about the adventures of both heroes and ordinary people. They often look to storytellers to provide answers to difficult questions and for interpretations of life's experiences. As we go through life, each of us gathers enough personal stories to fill many volumes of books.

About You

Sit with a partner in your class and prepare to share a favorite story. You can choose to tell a story popular in your native culture, or perhaps a story from your personal life. Spend twenty minutes exchanging stories with your partner. Take notes on what your partner tells you. After twenty minutes, join another pair of partners. Then each student tells the story that the other student told him/her. Then share some of these stories by telling them to the whole class.

Here are a few suggestions for story topics.

1. A popular folk tale from your country.
2. Your most embarrassing moment.
3. Your first impressions of the United States or of the country you are living in now.
4. A funny story about something that happened recently in your family.
5. Your best childhood memory.

Context Clues – A Way to Help You Understand Unfamiliar Vocabulary

What do you usually do when you read an unfamiliar English word or phrase? Do you reach for a dictionary? Ask a friend? Try to guess the meaning?

One popular method of figuring out the meanings of unfamiliar words is the use of context clues. Context clues are pieces of information or ideas that are related to the unfamiliar words or phrases. This information is usually found in the sentence that contains the new word or words, or in nearby surrounding sentences. The clues may be punctuation marks or specific words that provide hints or "clues" to meaning. Many students find that practice in recognizing context clues helps them figure out new vocabulary.

There are several forms of context clues. A sampling of four common context clues will be demonstrated in Chapters 1 and 2.

Context Clue # 1: Looking for definitions

When you see or hear an unfamiliar word, look or listen to see if the sentence already contains a definition of the word. Sentences containing definitions frequently include the word "means" or "meaning." In addition, definitions are often separated in a sentence by the use of commas or parentheses ( ). Check for commas or parentheses in a reading– or for specific pauses in a listening passage – that might be a clue for a definition.

1. Finding a definition if the sentence contains the clue word "meaning":

The policeman told the robber, "Freeze!," meaning "Don't move!"

What do you think the word *freeze* means? (Fill in your idea in the blank below.)

       I think the word *freeze* means _____.

2. Finding a definition if the sentence contains an explanation of a word after a comma:

The doctor said the patient needed to have a CAT Scan, a form of X-ray that takes measurements by the heat of the body.

What do you think a *CAT Scan* is?

       I think a *CAT Scan* is _____.

3. **Finding a definition if the sentence contains an explanation of a word inside parentheses ( ):**

When Bob realized he had a flat tire, he stopped the car and took out the jack (equipment used to lift the car off the ground).

What do you think a *jack* is?

I think a *jack* is _____.

Context Clue # 2: Looking for contrast, opposites, or difference with the words "but" and "however"

Look or listen for words like "but" and "however." These words often show a contrast or difference. If you are able to understand one part of the sentence containing a new word, it's likely that the new word means the opposite of the part of the sentence you already understand.

1. Finding a definition if the sentence contains the clue word "but":

Bill always had a lot of energy on rainy days, but his brother Bob always felt lethargic.

What do you think *lethargic* means?

I think *lethargic* means _____.

2. Finding a definition if the sentence contains the clue word "however":

Margo usually picks me up for work a few minutes late; however, today she was very punctual.

What do you think *punctual* means?

I think *punctual* means _____.

3. Finding a definition if the sentence contains the clue word "because."

The teacher asked us to make up a sentence by ourselves because it was better practice than copying from the text book.

What do you think *make up* means in this sentence?

I think *make up* means _____.

$\mathcal{V}$ocabulary Preview

Before listening to the first story on tape, it will be helpful to preview some of the vocabulary you will hear in the story. Previewing unfamiliar vocabulary words and idioms before listening to a chapter's essay can improve your general comprehension of the story and its events. Each Vocabulary Preview section in this book asks you to use the context clues described in this chapter and in chapter 2 to figure out the meanings of the new vocabulary words that appear in that chapter's essay.

The sentences below contain the new vocabulary words and phrases in this chapter's essay. Read the sentences carefully and try to figure out the meanings of the unfamiliar words by using context clues.

Example:

She likes to read tabloid newspapers, newspapers usually with small pages, many pictures, and very little serious news.

a. What are *tabloid newspapers?*

> I think tabloid newspapers are <u>newspapers usually with small pages, many pictures, and very little serious news.</u>

b. What context clue did you use?

> The context clue I used was <u>finding an explanation of a word after a comma.</u>

$\mathcal{Y}$our Turn

Fill in the lines below with the meaning of the word and also write the context clue you used to figure out your answer.

1. The priest was summoned (called) by the family to come quickly.

   a. I think the word *summoned* means _____

   _____.

   b. The context clue I used was _____

   _____.

2. The main fire in the house fire was out, but smoldering ashes from the bed were still very dangerous.

   a. I think the word *smoldering* means _____

   _____

   b. The context clue I used was _____

   _____.

3. They wrote his name, date of birth, and date of death on his tombstone (the headstone above the grave).

   a. I think the word *tombstone* means _____

   _____.

   b. The context clue I used was _____

   _____.

4.	According to the Bible, Adam and Eve were the first man and woman on the earth.

	a. I think *Adam and Eve* were_____

	_____.

	b. The context clue I used was _____

	_____.

5.	The lawyer asked us to suspend judgment (to wait until we hear the full story) before we decide which person robbed the store.

	a. I think a person who *suspends judgment* is a person who _____

	_____.

	b. The context clue I used was _____

	_____.

6.	Jane wanted to move to a house; however, she had to settle for living in an apartment until she saved more money.

	a. I think *settle for* means _____

	_____.

	b. The context clue I used was _____

	_____.

7.	My friend's behavior often takes him from the frying pan into the fire, meaning to go from one bad situation to a worse situation.

	a. I think *going from the frying pan into the fire* means _____

	_____.

	b. The context clue I used was _____

	_____.

Vocabulary Quick-Check Review

Check your understanding of the new words or phrases introduced in this chapter by completing the following matching exercise.

Write the letter of the definition in Column B that matches the word or phrase in Column A. Number 1 has been done as an example.

Column A	Column B
1. _b_ tabloid	a. to be called to come
2. _____ to be summoned	b. type of newspaper
3. _____ to suspend judgment	c. first man and woman, according to the Bible
4. _____ smoldering	d. from a bad situation to a worse situation
5. _____ settle	e. stone used to mark a person's grave in the cemetery
6. _____ out of the frying pan and into the fire	f. not giving your opinion immediately
7. _____ Adam and Eve	g. be satisfied with a compromise
8. _____ tombstone	h. slightly burning, with smoke

Essay Preview

One day Robert Fulghum read a newspaper story about a man rescued from a fire that had started in a burning bed. According to the newspaper, when the firemen asked the man what had happened, he gave them a very surprising answer. What do you think the man told them?

$\mathcal{F}$ocused Listening

Part 1

Look over the questions in each listening section before you listen to the tape. The questions will give you a general idea about the information contained in the essay. In addition, it will help you focus on the specific information needed to choose the best answer.

The listening exercises are divided into sections. The title of the chapter and the beginning of each listening section are announced by a speaker on the tape. Listen carefully and circle the best answer for each question.

When you've completed listening to Part 1, check your answers on the blackboard together as a whole class. If you wish, you may replay the complete tape—or just specific sections of it.

Example: The name of this chapter is
a. "Famous Fires."
b. "Why We Lay Down on Beds."
c. "It Was on Fire When I Lay Down on It."

The correct answer is "c." Circle letter "c."

SECTION I

1. The story about the man in the smoldering bed was
   a.   on TV.
   b.   in the newspaper.
   c.   in a magazine.

2. When the emergency squad asked the man what had happened, he said:
   a.   he had been smoking in bed.
   b.   a frying pan had caught fire.
   c.   it was on fire when he lay down on it.

SECTION II

3. According to Fulghum, the sentence "It was on fire when I lay down on it" is
   a.   a long sentence.
   b.   a life story in a sentence.
   c.   an untrue sentence.

4. Fulghum says that many of us could write the following sentence on our tombstone:
   a. "Hot water burns."
   b. "The devil made me do it."
   c. "I was looking for trouble, and I found it."

5. Fulghum's friend complained about his own lunch. Why did he complain?
   a. He always had the same lunch.
   b. He didn't feel hungry.
   c. He liked to complain about everything.

6. Who made his friend's lunch?
   a. his friend's wife.
   b. his friend.
   c. Fulghum.

SECTION III

7. Fulghum says that when we see other people do things,
   a. we usually don't know why they do them.
   b. it's easy to know why they do things.
   c. people always tell us why they do things.

8. Fulghum thinks the man in the burning bed might have been
   a. drunk.
   b. on vacation.
   c. out of work.

9. Fulghum says it's difficult to judge the man in the burning bed story because
   a. the man was injured in the fire.
   b. the man disappeared.
   c. we need to know much more information about what happened.

10. If we want to like our lives more, Fulghum suggests we should
    a. not lie on burning beds.
    b. suspend judgments.
    c. interview the man on the burning bed.

SECTION IV

11. Adam and Eve knew if they ate the piece of forbidden fruit, they
    a. would have a beautiful gift!
    b. would have a good dinner!
    c. would have trouble!

12. Fulghum says, "And you know the rest of the story" because, according to the Bible, after God warned Adam and Eve not to eat the forbidden fruit,
    a. they didn't eat the fruit.
    b. they couldn't find the fruit.
    c. they did eat the fruit.

Part 2

In this listening section, you will listen to the complete essay again, but this time there will be no pauses or narration in between each section.

The sentence below contain information about the essay you just heard. In every sentence, there is some information about the essay which is not true. The information which is not true is underlined. The sentences are listed in the order that the information is heard on the tape. As you listen to the essay again, cross out the incorrect information and write the correct information below it.

Example: This essay tells a story about a ~~woman~~ in a burning bed.
A man was in the burning bed.

1. Fulghum says the story about the man in the burning bed is not true.

   _____.

2. After the man was rescued from the burning bed, no one asked him how the fire started.

   _____.

3. Fulghum says that many people go looking for trouble, but very few people find it.

   _____.

4. Fulghum reported a conversation he had with his <u>wife</u>, who complained about having the same stuff in her lunch sack every day.

_____.

5. Fulghum says that when we see people do things, such as the man in the burning bed, it's <u>usually easy</u> to figure out why they do those things.

_____.

6. Fulghum says that we really don't <u>know</u> why the man rescued from the burning bed did what he did.

_____.

7. Fulghum says that the Bible says that God told Adam and Eve <u>to eat</u> that piece of fruit.

_____.

Listen to the tape again and check your answers with the rest of the class.

*W*hat Do You Think?

Discuss with your class the answers to the following questions.

1. Why do you think the man told the fireman the bed "was on fire when I lay down on it"? Do you really think he lay down on a burning bed? Do you think he told the truth, or did his words have a different meaning? What kind of person do you think he was?

2. Why did Fulghum use the colleague who complained about his lunch as an example of "out of the frying pan and into the fire"?

3. Fulghum says that many people could write one sentence to describe their life. He calls it "a life-story in a sentence." He suggests that the sentence describing the "life-story" of the man in the burning bed could be "out of the frying pan and into the fire." If you could write <u>one</u> sentence to describe your life or the life of someone you know, what sentence would it be?

Class Activity: Role Play

Pretend you are a newspaper reporter who is going to interview the man in the burning bed. What kind of information would you like to find out about him and his story? What things do you think the readers of your newspaper would like to know?

When newspaper reporters write stories, they try to get information that answers the questions Who? What? Where? Why? and How? Write at least one interview question using each of these question words.
Examples: <u>Who</u> was in the burning bed? <u>Why</u> did he lie down on it?

INTERVIEW QUESTIONS

1. Who _____?

2. What _____?

3. Where _____?

4. Why _____?

5. How _____?

Choose a student in your class to be the man or woman in the burning bed. Interview him or her with your questions and take notes on his or her answers. Organize the information into complete sentences. Then organize the sentences on notebook paper into one or two paragraphs for your newspaper report. Also, try to include two new vocabulary words from the Fulghum essay. After you write the story, be sure to add a title. Write the title here:

_____

Share the story with your class.

Reflections: A Cross-Cultural Issue for Discussion or Composition

Fulghum reminds us in this essay that the act of "jumping from the frying pan into the fire" is a very common behavior. Even though we know that the results of our actions will bring trouble, we often go ahead and do those actions anyway!

Can you remember a situation in your life (or in someone else's life) that you can describe as "jumping from the frying pan into the fire"? Prepare an oral presentation about your experience to share with the class, or write a composition on the same subject.

Dictation

Listen and fill in the missing words.

Oh, and one more thing. About the man in the _____ bed in the

story. As with most of what we see other people do, we really don't

know _____ they do it. If our own actions are _____ ,

how much so others? Why did he _____ down on the burning

bed? Was he _____? _____? Suicidal? _____?

Cold? Dumb? Did he just _____ a weird sense of humor? Or

what? I don't know. It's hard to _____ without a lot more

_____ . Oh sure, we go ahead and judge anyhow. But maybe if

judgment were _____ a bit more often, we would like us more.

God, it is _____, warned his first children, Adam and

_____. He made it _____. Don't eat that

_____ of fruit – it will lead to _____. You know the

rest of that story.

And part of the rest of that story is here in this tape.

Language of Culture: Ways to Ask Questions to Encourage Cultural Exchange

It is natural for new immigrants to be surprised and perhaps offended* by the cultural differences between their native land's customs and those of the United States. Immigrants often view these new cultural traditions by judging or evaluating them as "good" or "bad." In his essay "It Was on Fire When I Lay Down on It," Fulghum suggests that if we could "suspend judgment" – try to look at new situations without judging them – we could learn more and accept more easily the different traditions of the new culture.

The language we use to ask questions about things we see and/or don't understand in a new culture often shows if we are judging or accepting the new culture. It can be helpful to ask questions that create an exchange of cultural ideas instead of asking questions that may offend Americans.

Here is a conversation between Maria, an immigrant who recently arrived from Mexico, and her American friend Barbara. In this example, does Maria ask questions that might offend American culture, or do Maria's questions open up an exchange of ideas?

Maria: Why do American parents throw their teenagers out of their house when they become 18 years old?

Barbara: What? Can you explain what you mean?

Maria: Well, I've noticed that when American teenagers finish high school, they all leave home to go to a separate apartment or to go away to college. Why don't American parents love their children? In Mexico we always feel sad when our children leave to get married. It's so different with Americans.

*Offended—to feel insulted or embarrassed.

Maria got her opinions by observing American families in her neighborhood and also on TV. She saw many examples of teenagers moving out of the house to live on their own, but she was evaluating the situation by what it would mean in Mexico if a teenager moved out. The way she asked Barbara about the situation made Barbara upset. Maria seemed to be giving her opinion about it instead of asking for an explanation of it.

Let's look at Maria's conversation with Barbara when she asks the same question in a way that invites cultural exchange.

Maria: Barbara, I've noticed that many American teenagers leave home as soon as they finish high school or become 18 years old. This is very strange to me because in Mexico children stay home until they are married. What's the reason for this?

Barbara: Oh, you know that American parents try to develop indepen dence in their children. They are very sad when their children leave home, but it also means they have been successful par ents. Being able to live on your own is very important in American culture. Also, some teenagers move to other cities and states to go to college because there may not be a college near their homes or because they want to find a job somewhere else.

Maria: Oh, now I see. I thought the parents threw them out! That was really a big misunderstanding!

Notice that Maria opened the second conversation with *I've noticed that* and later asked *What's the reason?* Do you know other polite ways to ask questions about a new culture?

Here are two more examples of opening phrases for questions about cultural differences.

"What does it mean when (American teenagers leave home early)?"

"Is it OK if (teenagers leave their home, or does it mean there is a problem in their family)?"

$\mathcal{P}$ractice

Make a list of five things you'd like to ask about U.S. culture. Then create a question using one new phrase. Choose one polite phrase for the question you create for each situation.

Situation: Americans are always smiling.

Question: *What's the reason* Americans smile so often?

Situation: Teenagers leave home when they're 18 years old.

Question: *What does it mean* when U.S. teenagers leave home when they're 18 years old?

1. **Situation:** _____

   Polite question: *What does it mean when* _____?

2. **Situation:** _____

   Polite question: *Is it OK if* _____?

3. **Situation:** _____

   Polite question: *What's the reason* _____?

4. **Situation:** _____

   Polite question: _____?

5. **Situation:** _____

   Polite question: _____?

Chapter 2

**THE
MERMAID**

$\mathcal{M}$uch of the creative energy that produces an individual's ideas and beliefs depends upon imagination. A good example of this is a magic show. The magician uses tricks from his imagination and depends on the imagination of the audience to be surprised and enjoy the show. Imagination provides the basics for great ideas in technology as well as the personal creativity in our everyday lives.

Look at the illustration on this page.

- What objects or symbols are in the picture?
- In what ways do the illustration and the quotation above it require you to use your imagination?
- What clues in the picture give you some ideas about the essay in this chapter?

Share your ideas and imagination with your partner.

About Imagination

In several instances in the Saint-Exupéry story The Little Prince, the writer demonstrates his belief that children and adults look at the world in different ways. In general, he thinks that the adults see things in very practical, useful ways and rarely use their imagination. Children, Saint-Exupéry writes, see things usually through their imagination. Here's an example.

> Grown-ups love figures.* When you tell them that you have made a friend, they never ask you any questions about essential matters.** They never say to you, "What does his voice sound like? What games does he love best? Does he collect butterflies?" Instead, they demand: "How old is he? How many brothers has he? How much does he weigh? How much money does his father make?" Only from these figures do they think they have learned anything about him.

About You

What are your ideas about Saint-Exupéry's observations? Do you agree or disagree with his conclusion about the differences between children and adults? Do you think these differences are important or unimportant?

With a partner, talk about Saint-Exupéry's main idea in the above paragraph from The Little Prince and answer the following questions.

1. What does the paragraph say about the differences between the ways adults and children think about "a new friend"? Do you agree or disagree with Saint-Exupéry about this?

2. What do people think about imagination in your culture? Is it encouraged? If so, is it encouraged in children? Is it also encouraged in adults? Explain your answers.

*Figures—numbers and statistics.
**Essential— most important.

3. In what ways do you express your imagination in the things you do every day? Give at least three examples.

4. Now that you have done these beginning exercises, use your imagination and try to guess what this chapter's essay is about! Share your ideas with your partner.

$\mathcal{M}$ore About Context Clues

In Chapter 1 you read about two techniques to use context clues for finding the meaning of unfamiliar vocabulary words. Here are two additional suggestions for using context clues.

Context Clue # 3 : "Looking for the word "because."

The word "because" usually shows a reason for things. If you understand the reason for things, it is sometimes possible to figure out the meaning of nearby unfamiliar words.

1. Finding a definition if the sentence contains the clue word "because":

Maria went to bed early tonight because she was worn out from working so many hours on the job.

What do you think *worn out* means?

I think *worn out* means _____.

The teacher asked us to make up a sentence by ourselves because it was better practice than copying from the text book.

What do you think *make up* means in this sentence?

I think *make up* means _____.

Context Clue # 4 : Looking for examples or explanations with the words "such as" or "like."

Sometimes examples or explanations of those words that are unfamiliar to you appear in the sentence or in nearby sentences. They are usually preceded by the words "such as" or "like."

1. Finding a definition if the sentence contains the clue words "such as":

Bob does reckless things when he drives, such as speeding and going through red lights.

What do you think *reckless* means in this sentence?

I think *reckless* means _____ .

2. Finding a definition by the use of the word "like":

Tan likes to eat pungent food like hot peppers and hot mustard.

What do you think *pungent* means in this sentence?

I think *pungent* means _____ .

You have seen four common examples of context clues. What other ways do you use to try to figure out the meanings of new words and phrases? Share your techniques with the class. Have the suggestions written on the blackboard and write them all down in your notebook to practice throughout this English program.

*V*ocabulary Preview Through Context Clues

Before listening to the story about imagination, it will be helpful to preview some of the vocabulary you will hear in the story. Previewing unfamiliar vocabulary words and idioms before listening to each chapter's essay can improve your general comprehension of the story and the events in it.

The sentences below contain new vocabulary words and phrases in this chapter's essay. Read the sentences carefully and try to figure out the meaning of the unfamiliar words by using context clues. Fill in the line below each sentence.

1. The players on the football team often huddle (move into a small, tight group) to exchange secret signals for the game.

   I think that *huddle* means _____.

2. Mermaids are popular in children's stories because they create a wonderful fantasy about a woman who is part human and part fish.

   I think that a *mermaid* is_____.

3. The kids wanted to play an active running game such as football or "Giants, Wizards and Dwarfs."

   I think that *"Giants, Wizards and Dwarfs"** is _____

   _____.

4. Her parents were busy doing "parenty" things, like going to work, cleaning the house, and doing food shopping.

   I think that *"parenty"* things are _____

   _____.

5. The child made a tug (a small pull) at her father's sleeve because she wanted him to know that she wanted to leave the party.

   I think that a *tug* is _____.

6. Apples are in the category of fruit, but onions are in the category of vegetables.

   I think that *category* means _____ .

*Giant—an extremely large and tall imaginary human or other creature.
 Wizard—an imaginary person who can do magic.
 Dwarf—an undersized, very short person, real or imaginary.

7. When the game was ready to begin, he mustered his troops (which means he brought all the children together in one place) and explained the rules.

I think that *mustered his troops* means _____

_____.

8. The president fired three workers because their lazy behavior didn't fit into the scheme of things at the company.

I think that *fit into the scheme of things* means _____

_____.

9. Whenever I feel upset, I visit my mother because I take it for granted that she will listen to me and help me.

I think that to *take something for granted* means _____

_____.

10. Nancy had so many interesting parts to her personality that it is hard to describe her with the usual pigeonholes (narrow descriptions).

I think that *pigeonhole* means _____

_____.

11. The original play was only thirty minutes long; however, the director wrote a large-scale version of the original play that took over two hours to perform.

I think that a *large-scale version of something* is _____

_____.

12. She showed great dignity (personal value) when she accepted the award for service to the community.

I think that *dignity* means _____

_____.

Vocabulary Quick-Check Review

Check your understanding of the new vocabulary words and phrases introduced in this chapter by completing the following matching exercise. Write the letter of the definition in Column B that matches the word or phrase in Column A.

Column A	Column B
1. _____ "Giants, Wizards, and Dwarfs"	a. small spaces or narrow descriptions
2. _____ large-scale version	b. imaginary creature that is half woman and half fish
3. _____ huddle	c. stand together in a secret group
4. _____ category	d. personal value
5. _____ mermaid	e. bring everyone together in one place
6. _____ tug	f. have the same ideas and do the same things as most others in a group
7. _____ dignity	g. childrens' game
8. _____ muster one's troops	h. a bigger copy
9. _____ take for granted	i. group of similar objects or ideas
10. _____ "parenty" things	j. small pull
11. _____ pigeonholes	k. expect to get something automatically
12. _____ fit into the scheme of things	l. common things parents do

*E*ssay Preview

Have you ever supervised forty children at one time? Fulghum was in charge of forty kids one day while their parents were busy. Because there were so many kids, he decided to play a game that would include everyone in the group. The game was "Giants, Wizards, and Dwarfs." In this game there are three teams—the Giants, the Wizards, and the Dwarfs. Each child decides which team he or she wants to be on.

There are rules and procedures that decide which is the winning team, and Fulghum originally thought that each child would be happy to play the game by the rules. But he got a big surprise, and he had to use his imagination to deal with the situation. What surprise do you think he had?

*F*ocused Listening

Part 1

Look over the questions in each listening section before you listen to the tape. The questions will give you a general idea about the information contained in the essay. In addition, it will help you focus on the specific information needed to choose the best answer.

The listening exercises are divided into sections. The titles of the chapter and the beginning of each listening section are announced by a speaker on the tape. Listen carefully and circle the best answer for each question.

When you've completed listening to Part 1, check your answers on the blackboard together as a whole class. If you wish, you may replay the complete tape—or just specific sections of it.

SECTION I

1. What was the name of the game Fulghum played with the kids?
   a. Frogs, Pumpkins and Tigers.
   b. Giants, Wizards, and Dwarfs.
   c. Giants, Fairies, and Dwarfs.

2. He was taking care of all these children because
   a. their parents needed time to take care of "parenty" things.
   b. he enjoyed military games.
   c. he enjoyed imaginary creatures.

3. Fulghum mustered his troops and
   a. took a walk.
   b. explained the game.
   c. went outside.

4. This game is a large-scale version of
   a. baseball.
   b. football.
   c. rock, paper, and scissors.

5. In this game,
   a. every player makes decisions.
   b. no players make decisions.
   c. only the leader makes decisions.

6. Fulghum says the real purpose of the game is to
   a. run around and keep score exactly.
   b. run around and chase people until everyone forgets which side he or she is on.
   c. run around and hide.

SECTION II

7. In this game, children decide
   a. whether to be a giant, a wizard, or a dwarf.
   b. how long to play the game.
   c. the name of the game.

8. While the groups huddled,
   a. a tug came at Fulghum's jacket and sleeve.
   b. a tug came at Fulghum's pant leg.
   c. a tug came at Fulghum's coat.

9. A small child was standing there, who asked,
   a. "Where do the giants stand?"
   b. "Where do the wizards stand?"
   c. "Where do the mermaids stand?"

10. Fulghum told the little girl
    a. he's seen a lot of mermaids.
    b. there are no such things as mermaids.
    c. he had never heard of mermaids.

11. Fulghum was surprised the girl asked to be a mermaid because
    a. kids run a lot, and mermaids only swim.
    b. kids wouldn't recognize a mermaid.
    c. kids usually choose to be a giant or a wizard or a dwarf.

SECTION III

12. The little girl didn't relate to being
    a. a mermaid.
    b. a dwarf or giant.
    c. an elephant.

13. The little girl believed that
    a. mermaids should be allowed to play the game.
    b. Fulghum could not help her.
    c. there were too many children playing the game.

14. She felt proud of being a mermaid and
    a. didn't think she should have to leave the game because mermaids never played before.
    b. thought she should leave the game to let everyone know she was a mermaid.
    c. asked Fulghum if she could leave the game.

15. Fulghum realized she wanted to participate
    a. if he would call her name.
    b. wherever mermaids fit into the scheme of things.
    c. if the kids would not recognize her.

16. Fulghum thought she had a lot of
    a. dignity.
    b. fear.
    c. humor.

17. Fulghum thought her question was important because he thinks
    a. she speaks very well.
    b. he wants to build a school.
    c. we should always pay attention to everyone's ideas and imagination.

SECTION IV

18. How did Fulghum feel when he decided to find a special place in the game for a mermaid?
    a. He felt the other children would be angry.
    b. He felt she was too small to be a mermaid.
    c. He felt he did the right thing.

19. He told the little girl that mermaids stand
    a. next to the giants.
    b. by the dwarfs and wizards.
    c. by the King of the Sea.

20. Who was the King of the Sea?
    a. One of the children.
    b. Fulghum.
    c. One of the other parents.

21. He said mermaids are real because
    a. he has seen them in the ocean.
    b. he has held the hand of a mermaid.
    c. you can read books about them.

Part 2

In this listening section, you will listen to the complete essay again, but this time there will be no pauses or narration in between each section.

The sentences below contain information about the essay you just heard. In every sentence, there is some information about the essay which is not true. The information which is not true is underlined. The sentences are listed in the order that the information is heard on the tape. As you listen to the essay again, cross out the incorrect information and write the correct information below it.

1. "Giants, Wizards, and Dwarfs" is the name of a famous <u>football</u> game.

_____.

2. Fulghum was left in charge of about <u>eighty (80)</u>.

_____.

3. The purpose of the game he played was <u>to sit quietly and paint</u> pictures.

_____.

4. The little girl who tugged at his pants leg asked Fulghum where <u>the showmen</u> stand.

   _____.

5. Mermaids <u>have always been</u> part of the game "Giants, Wizards, and Dwarfs."

   _____.

6. Fulghum was <u>not surprised</u> that the girl said she was a mermaid.

   _____.

7. Fulghum told the girl that mermaids stand next to him, the King of the <u>country</u>.

   _____.

8. Fulghum says that mermaids <u>do not exist</u>.

   _____.

Listen to the tape again and check your answers with the rest of the class.

*W*hat Do You Think?

Discuss with your class the answers to the following questions.

1. Why was Fulghum surprised by the little girl's request to be a mermaid?
2. How did Fulghum solve her problem?

3. If you were Fulghum, what would you tell the little girl who said she was a mermaid? Would you tell her there were no mermaids in this game and that she would have to choose to be either a giant, wizard, or dwarf? Or would you follow Fulghum's example and create a special group just for mermaids? Explain your answer.

4. In his introduction to his book *It Was on Fire When I Lay Down on It*, Fulghum writes that he believes "imagination is stronger than knowledge." What do you think he means?

Class Activity

Teach your class or group a game that is popular in your country. It can be a game for children or for adults, and it can be played by one or many players. After you explain the procedure, have all the students in your class or group join in and play the game.

Fill out the following form to organize your ideas about your game:

a. What's the name of the game?

_____.

b. How many players are there?

_____.

c. Is it for adults or children?

_____.

d. Where do you play it?

_____.

e. Do you need any special equipment?

_____.

f. How do you win the game?

_____.

$\mathcal{R}$eflections: A Cross-Cultural Issue for Discussion or Composition

Americans call children's stories with imaginary creatures "fairy tales." Usually the stories tell about the adventures of these imaginary creatures, and they are used to entertain or instruct children.

In this essay, children were introduced to a few very popular fairy tale creatures in western civilization—mermaids, giants, wizards, and dwarfs. What imaginary creatures are popular in your culture? Why do you think they are popular?

Think about the fairy tales you knew when you were a child. Is there one story that influenced you or that you'll always remember? What was the story? In what ways does this story reflect the attitudes or beliefs of your culture?

Prepare an oral presentation or write a composition about this story or a story from your life to share with your class. Show how the story reflects the ideas of your own culture.

$\mathcal{D}$ictation

Listen and fill in the missing words.

She did not relate to being a _____ a Wizard, or a _____. She

knew her category. _____. And was not about to leave the

_____ and go over and _____ against the wall where a

_____ would stand. She intended to _____, wherever

Mermaids _____ into the scheme of things. Without giving up

_____ or identity. She _____ it for granted that there was a

_____ for Mermaids and that I would know just where.

Well, where _____ the Mermaids stand? All the "Mermaids" — all

those who are _____, who do not _____ _____

_____ and who do not accept the available boxes and _____?

Answer that question and you can _____ a school, a _____,

or a _____ on it.

Language of Culture: Ways to Ask Someone to Repeat What Was Said

When the young girl in "The Mermaid" essay first asked Fulghum "Where do the Mermaids stand?," Fulghum was very surprised and repeated what she said to be sure he had heard her correctly.

Girl:	Where do the Mermaids stand?
Fulghum:	Where do the Mermaids stand?

In U.S. culture, it is expected that people ask questions to check that they understand what someone said to them. At work in particular, your boss or supervisor will expect you to ask each time you are not sure about something he or she said. In fact, using techniques to be sure you understand what someone said to you can prevent what happened to Magda, a student from Egypt, on her first job.

Magda had been working in a local office, for a month, and she liked her job. One day, she came to class very upset, and we asked her what had happened. She told us she had been fired. "Why?" we all asked.

Magda:	Because I didn't follow all of my supervisor's orders.
Class:	Why not?
Magda:	So many times I wasn't sure what she wanted me to do.
Class:	Why didn't you tell her when you didn't understand something?
Magda:	She would be angry at me if I asked.

Student:	Did you ever tell her when you didn't understand her?
Magda:	No, never.
Student:	So how can she know you don't understand?
Magda:	She wants me to know everything. She expects me to know.
Student:	In Egypt, do you ever ask your boss to explain something?
Magda:	Never. He would be insulted. I would ask another worker to help me, but never the boss.
Student:	Magda, here in the U.S., the boss expects you to ask questions. In most situations, Americans ask you to explain something if they don't understand.
Magda:	I didn't know that. I really misunderstood. I'll know what to do the next time.

Has anything like this ever happened to you? If so, what did you do?

There are many ways to ask for repetition in English. Like Fulghum, you can repeat the thing someone said in a questioning voice:

Supervisor:	Take these books to Mr. Liang.
Worker:	Take these books to Mr. Liang?

Another useful technique is to use specific questions or statements that show that you are asking for repetition. Some of the most common:

> What did you say?
> Would you mind repeating that?
> I'm not following you.
> I didn't catch what you said.
> Pardon me?

The following examples illustrate how you can use these questions and statements to clarify what has been said to you.

Mark:	I'll be home by 10:30 tonight.
Joanne:	You'll be home by 10:30 tonight?

Judi:	The book needs five more illustrations.
Stan:	I didn't catch what you said.
Judi:	I said the book needs five more illustrations.

Kay:	Which restaurant should we have the party in?
Bill:	What did you say?
Kay:	Which restaurant should we have the party in?

Max:	How many days will we be in California?
Lucille:	I'm not following you.
Max:	I said, "How many days will we be in California?"

Mildred:	What's the best time for me to call you?
Jack:	Pardon me?
Mildred:	What's the best time for me to call you?

𝒫ractice

With a partner, practice asking for repetition by repeating what the person has said or by using one of the following questions or statements.

Pardon me?
Would you mind repeating that?
What did you say?
I'm not following you.
I didn't catch what you said.

Examples:

1. Student A: Do you know what time the plane leaves?

   Student B: (Choose one of the above statements or questions.)

   Student A: Do you know what time the plane leaves?

2. Student A: I think we should start working on our project today.

   Student B: (Choose one of the above statements or questions.)

   Student A: I said that I think we should start working on our project today.

"Man is made of dreams and bones."
—David Mallett, from "Garden Song"

Chapter 3

THE GOOD STUFF

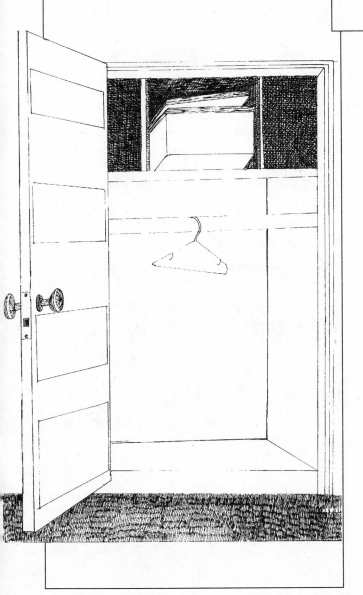

*E*ach of us has memories and souvenirs of special moments in our lives. Some of us keep these treasures secret, and other people show them and easily talk about them.

Look at the picture on this page.

- What does it suggest about the story in this chapter?
- What images come to your mind?
- In what way do you think the quotation above the picture is related to the picture?

Share your ideas with a partner.

About Memories

Writers have filled libraries with books and poems about memories since the earliest days of writing. Whether the memories recorded are about the author or about someone else, the subject of memories has remained a very popular one. Cicero, a popular Roman writer in the first century, expressed this very common view about memory when he wrote that "Memory is the treasury . . . of all things."*

Memory has also been recognized as a tool for personal growth and understanding. By using our memories to analyze and evaluate our past experiences, we gain understanding about our present and future.

About You

Our thoughts and feelings about the things we remember can lift our spirits in many ways and often take us back to an earlier time in our life. Do you have any memories about a time in your life that always brings special thoughts and pleasures as you remember them? Sit with your partner and share your memories and ideas by asking the following questions.

1. What are some of your favorite memories?

2. Do you have a souvenir or special object that you always keep with you? If yes, what is it and why is it so special to you?

3. What special thing did you take with you when you left your country? What special thing did you <u>not</u> take with you but you now wish you had?

Vocabulary Preview Through Context Clues

Before listening to the "Good Stuff" story, it will be helpful to preview some of the vocabulary words you will hear in the story.

*Treasury—a storage place for valuable things.

Previewing unfamiliar vocabulary words and idioms before listening to each chapter's essay can improve your general comprehension of the story and its events.

The sentences below contain new vocabulary words and phrases in this chapter's essay. Read the sentences carefully and try to figure out the meanings of the new words by using context clues. Write your ideas about the meanings on the line below the sentence.

1. Before my mother died, she gave me her favorite ring, and it has become the most important keepsake (souvenir) in my life.

   I think a *keepsake* is _____.

2. Immediately after the kitten was born, her mother lifted it gingerly (gently) in her mouth and moved it to a safe place.

   I think gingerly means _____.

3. Lisa's mother asked her to change her old pants because they were ratty and full of holes.

   I think *ratty* means _____.

4. I have to hustle off to the bus stop because I don't want to miss my bus.

   I think *hustle off* means _____.

5. No one helped Jo Anne clean up after the party, so she was left holding the bag.

   I think if someone is *left holding the bag*, it means that _____

   _____.

6. When they cleaned up the closet, they found many odds and ends like papers, clothes, gifts, and photos from their life together.

   I think *odds and ends are* _____

   _____.

7. When we asked Jim what his favorite sport is, he said, "Tennis is my bag" because he likes tennis a lot.

I think if something is *your bag*, it means that _____

_____ .

8. The company always screens job applications carefully because it wants to be sure of each person's qualifications before he or she comes in for an interview.

I think *to screen* something means _____

_____ .

9. Bill worked in the mail room and had many responsibilities, such as sorting out the mail and then delivering it to each department.

I think *sorting out* something means _____

_____ .

10. Before he threw out the letter, he wadded it up in his palm because he felt so angry.

I think that *wadding something up* means _____

_____ .

11. Larry repaired the wire with duct tape because it repairs electrical wires very well.

I think that *duct tape* is _____

_____ .

12. The mother told her fighting children that she didn't want to hold court, which means to decide who was right and who was wrong.

I think *to hold court* means _____ .

_____ .

13. I think that the idiom "standing knee-deep in the river and dying of thirst" means that the thing you are looking for is right in front of you, but you don't see it.

I think that *standing knee-deep in the river and dying of thirst* means _____

_____ .

$\mathcal{V}$ocabulary Quick-Check Review

Check your understanding of the new words and phrases introduced in this chapter by completing the following matching exercise. Write the letter of the definition in Column B that matches the word or phrase in Column A.

Column A	Column B
1. _____ duct tape	a. very carefully
2. _____ gingerly	b. I like it a lot
3. _____ ratty	c. mixture of things
4. _____ a keepsake	d. to find out who is right or wrong
5. _____ screen	e. folded or pushed into the shape of a ball
6. _____ sort out	f. leave in a hurry
7. _____ hustle off	g. look through something to evaluate what's there
8. _____ be left holding the bag	h. a souvenir
9. _____ be standing knee-deep in the water and dying of thirst	i. describing something in poor condition
10. _____ It's "my bag."	j. electrical tape
11. _____ wadded up	k. having something, but not seeing it
12. _____ to hold court	l. be left with all the responsibilities
13. _____ odds and ends	m. organize a pile or group of things

*E*ssay Preview

In the following essay, Mr. Fulghum introduces us to a special souvenir–a cardboard box he calls the "good stuff." He tells us that no matter where he has moved or how many times he has planned to throw
away all his junk, he keeps this box and its contents. The box is so
important to him that if his house should ever catch on fire, the box
"goes with me when I run."

Can you guess what's in the box?

*F*ocused Listening

Part 1

Look over the questions in each listening section before you listen to the
tape. The questions will give you a general idea about the information
contained in the essay. In addition, it will help you focus on the specific
information needed to choose the best answer.

The listening exercises are divided into sections. The title of the chapter
and the beginning of each listening section are announced by a speaker
on the tape. Listen carefully and circle the best answer for each question.

When you've completed listening to Part 1, check your answers on the
blackboard together as a whole class. If you wish, you may replay the
complete tape—or just specific sections of it.

SECTION I

1. The cardboard box is stored
   a. on a high shelf in the studio.
   b. in the basement.
   c. in the trunk of the car.

2. The box contains
   a. old clothes.
   b. newspapers.
   c. personal treasures.

3. Fulghum says a thief looking into the box would not take anything because
   a. the box was messy.
   b. the box was difficult to carry.
   c. the box didn't contain anything worth a lot of money.

4. One of the keepsakes in the box is
   a. a necklace.
   b. a small paper bag.
   c. a watch.

SECTION II

5. The lunch sack has belonged to him
   a. a short time.
   b. since he was young.
   c. fourteen years.

6. He usually received a paper sack from Molly in the morning because
   a. she often made the lunches.
   b. she was an artist.
   c. Fulghum asked for the sack.

7. Molly usually put these things in the lunch bag:
   a. fried chicken sandwiches and cookies.
   b. pizza, a note, and milk money.
   c. sandwiches, apples, milk money, and a note or a treat.

8. This morning was different because Molly handed Fulghum
   a. a chocolate cake.
   b. two bags.
   c. one bag and an apple.

9. When Fulghum asked Molly what was in the bag,
   a. she didn't tell him.
   b. she laughed.
   c. she cried.

SECTION III

10. When Fulghum started to eat his lunch,
    a. he shook all the contents out of Molly's bag.
    b. he sat on Molly's bag.
    c. he put Molly's bag in his drawer.

11. Fulghum found the following in Molly's paper sack:
    a. two chocolate kisses and a plastic dinosaur.
    b. three big stones and a big seashell.
    c. a pen and ten marbles.

12. Why did Fulghum throw out the sack?
    a. He thought there was nothing he needed in it.
    b. It messed up his desk.
    c. It had a hole in it.

SECTION IV

13. That night Molly asked Fulghum,
    a. "Where's the apple?"
    b. "Where's the milk money?"
    c. "Where's my bag?"

14. When Molly found out that Fulghum didn't have the bag,
    a. she laughed and said it was okay.
    b. she was upset and started to cry.
    c. she left the room.

15. The note Molly put in the bag said:
    a. Don't forget to take this sack.
    b. Save me the chocolate kisses.
    c. I love you.

16. Fulghum said "uh-oh" because he realized
    a. he had eaten Molly's chocolate kisses and he felt sorry about it.
    b. the bag was really a very important thing to Molly, and he had thrown it out.
    c. it was time to eat dinner, and he was hungry.

17. Fulghum said he felt his "daddy permit" had run out because
    a. he had done something to hurt his daughter.
    b. he forgot to renew it.
    c. he would not be permitted to have more children.

SECTION V

18. Fulghum felt it was a long trip back to the office because
    a. it was so far away.
    b. he was so worried about finding the sack.
    c. it was late at night.

19. The janitor wanted to help Fulghum because
    a. he had children, too.
    b. that was his job.
    c. he wanted to be sure that he didn't steal something.

20. Fulghum and the janitor
    a. didn't find the bag.
    b. gave up looking for the bag.
    c. found the bag and the stuff inside the bag..

SECTION VI

21. Fulghum cleaned up all the stuff in the bag and carried it home "gingerly" because
    a. he wanted to protect all Molly's special treasures.
    b. it was so heavy.
    c. he thought about his cat.

22. After dinner Fulghum asked Molly to
    a. tell the story of each thing.
    b. forget about the bag.
    c. put the bag away.

23. Molly's stories took
    a. a short time to tell.
    b. a long time to tell.
    c. an hour to tell.

24. When Molly explained the story attached to each object in the bag, Fulghum realized
    a. each thing had a special meaning to her.
    b. she had great language ability.
    c. she wanted him to eat the chocolate kisses.

SECTION VII

25. Molly gave the bag back to Fulghum several times
    a. because he had been good.
    b. for no apparent reason.
    c. when he asked for it.

26. Fulghum wanted Molly to give him the bag, so he
    a. asked her for it.
    b. took it.
    c. tried to be good.

27. Fulghum felt he had been "standing knee-deep in the river and dying of thirst." This means
    a. he was always thirsty.
    b. he had love all around him and couldn't see it.
    c. he will die from thirst.

28. Molly just stopped giving him the bag one day because she
    a. forgot about it.
    b. threw it out.
    c. grew up.

29. When Fulghum says "It's my bag now," he means
    a he owns the bag.
    b. he won't be blind to love and affection again.
    c. Molly doesn't want it back.

Part 2

In this listening section, you will listen to the complete essay again, but this time there will be no pauses or narration in between each section.

The sentences below contain information about the essay you just heard. In every sentence, there is some information about the essay which is not true. The information which is not true is underlined. The sentences are listed in the order that the information is heard on the tape. As you listen to the essay again, cross out the incorrect information and write the correct information below it.

1. Fulghum keeps all his "good stuff" in a metal box in his closet.

   _____.

2. Fulghum says that any thief looking into his "good stuff" box would be happy to take everything inside it.

   _____.

3. A small <u>paper doll</u> is one of the items in the "good stuff" box.

   _____.

4. Fulghum has this paper sack left over from the days his <u>son</u> made lunches for school and work.

   _____.

5. At lunchtime when Fulghum opened the sack, he found a lunch <u>but nothing else</u>.

   _____.

6. When Fulghum returned home for dinner, his daughter <u>never asked</u> about the paper sack.

   _____.

7. Fulghum had to return to his office because he had left his <u>briefcase</u> there.

   _____.

8. Fulghum <u>did not find</u> all the things from the paper sack in the trash can at his office.

   _____.

9. Molly told Fulghum the story about <u>one</u> thing in the paper sack.

   _____.

10. Fulghum <u>didn't learn</u> any lessons from his experience with the paper lunch sack.

   _____.

Listen to the tape again and check your answers with the rest of the class.

*W*hat Do You Think?

Discuss with your class the answers to the following questions.

1. Why was the box on the top shelf so important to Fulghum? Where do <u>you</u> keep special things with important memories?

2. When Fulghum opened up the lunch sack Molly gave him, he ate the lunch and threw away the rest of the stuff in the sack. Why did he throw those things away?

3. If you were Fulghum and you found out that you had thrown away your daughter's souvenirs, what would you do? Would you go back to your office as Fulghum did, or would you do something else?

*C*lass Activities

1. Bring to class a very special keepsake of your own and tell the class the story attached to it.

2. Tell the class a story that really happened to you when you were "left holding the bag."

3. Tell the class a story describing a time in your life when you or someone you know was "standing knee-deep in the river and dying of thirst."

*R*eflections: A Cross-Cultural Issue for Discussion or Composition

The role* of the father is very different from culture to culture. In the "Good Stuff" essay, Fulghum talks about his "daddy permit."** He feels that the respect and honor he gets from his children are things he must earn, not be given automatically.

Is this idea of the father similar to or different from the idea of the father in your culture? What do you think about Fulghum's view of his role as a father?

---

*Role — your purpose or duty in society.

**Daddy permit — funny phrase Fulghum created about behavior for a father.

Prepare an oral presentation about your ideas concerning the role of the father in your culture, or write a composition about the same subject and share it with the class.

$\mathcal{D}$ictation

Listen and fill in the missing words.

To my _____ , Molly gave the bag to me once again _____ days later. Same _____ bag. Same _____ inside. I felt _____ . And _____ . And _____ . And a little more comfort-able wearing the _____ of Father. Over several _____ the bag went with me from time to time. It was never _____ to me why I did or did not get it on a given day. I began to think of it as the _____ _____ , and I tried to be good the night before so I might be _____ it the next morning.

In time Molly _____ her attention to other _____ . . . found other treasures . . . lost _____ in the game . . . _____ up. Something. _____ ? I was left _____ ____ _____ . She gave it to me one morn-ing and never _____ for its return. And so I have it _____ .

Sometimes I think of all the times in this _____ life when I must have _____ the affection I was being given. A friend calls this "standing knee-deep in the river and dying of thirst."

So the worn paper sack is there in the _____ on the shelf, left over

from a time when a child said "Here—this is the _____ I've got. Take

it—it's _____. Such as I have, give I to thee."

I _____ it the first time. But it's my _____ now.

*L*anguage of Culture: Ways to Use and Recognize Feedback

In the "Good Stuff" essay, Fulghum lets his daughter know he is listening carefully to her explanation about the things in the paper bag by saying "I see." Using phrases like "I see," "oh," and "uh-huh" is called "giving feedback." Feedback is also found in body movements such as nodding, shaking one's head, and smiling.

Learning to recognize and use feedback are important parts of communication in the United States–at home, at work, or anywhere in the community. Here is a true story that shows the important role of feedback in U.S. culture:

Tesfay is a student from Ethiopia. He got a job as a janitor in a local hospital after he had been in the U.S. a few months. The first day on his job, he did everything his supervisor told him to do, and he thought everything was okay.

The next day, the head of Personnel asked him to report to his office. Tesfay couldn't imagine what was wrong.

Personnel Manager:	What's wrong? Don't you like your job?
Tesfay:	Excuse me. I don't understand.
Personnel Manager:	Your supervisor complained about you yesterday. He said you never answered him when he spoke to you and you never smiled.
Tesfay:	Never smile?
Personnel Manager:	Yes. Don't you like your job?
Tesfay:	I do like it! Was I supposed to smile? When the supervisor told me to do something, I did it. Did he complain about my work?
Personnel Manager:	No, the work was okay. He complained about your attitude. He said you don't care about your job.

What happened to Tesfay?

In Ethiopia, if your supervisor speaks to you, you keep quiet. You don't ask questions or respond in any other way. Here in the United States, supervisors and co-workers (and even friends) will expect you to use some form of "feedback"–verbal or body language–when they speak to you. They think that using feedback shows that you care or understand them because you are listening carefully to what they say.

$\mathcal{P}$air Practice

Interview a classmate and ask the following questions.

1. Is the use of feedback techniques common in your culture? Verbal? Body language?

2. When are these techniques used? At home? At work? In the community? (Share examples of feedback techniques, telling where and how you use them.)

3. Pretend you are telling a partner about an experience you had recently. Your partner should listen carefully and use feedback techniques–verbal or body language–to let you know he or she is listening and understanding everything you say. He or she should use expressions such as "uh-huh," "sure," "okay," "oh," "I see," and "I understand."

You can begin the conversation with: "I had a really unusual experience yesterday." Here are a few other suggestions:

a. You had a flat tire last night at 10 o'clock on your way home from English class.

b. Your friends gave you a surprise birthday party last week.

c. You won $500 in the lottery.

d. You had a strange dream last night.

e. You ate Mexican food for the first time today.

"To everything there is a season."
    —Ecclesiastes

Chapter 4

RITES OF PASSAGE

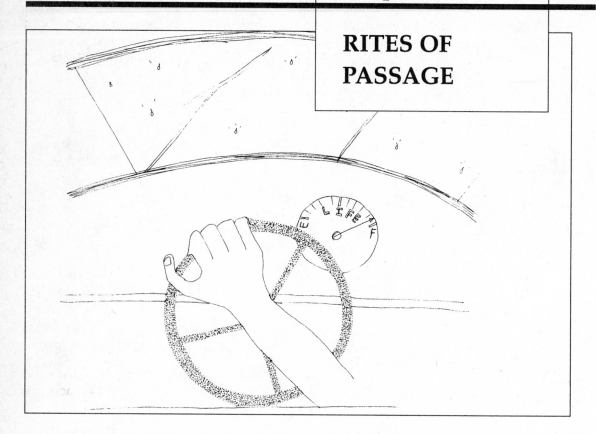

*I*t is common in many cultures to mark an individual's passing through the seasons of life—such as birth, marriage and death—with special customs and ceremonies. Many of these times are celebrated publicly, such as in weddings and funerals. Other seasons in our lives—such as the first time you fall in love or the first difficult decisions you face—are often marked privately. All these special times and movements in life's journey are commonly called "rites of passage."

The illustration on this page shows one very popular activity in some countries that often begins in the teenage years.

- What activity is this?
- Is this a popular activity for teenagers in your country?
- Look carefully at the illustration. In what ways does the picture show that this is a "rite of passage"?

Share your ideas with a partner.

$\mathcal{A}$bout Rites of Passage

One rite of passage that is common to many cultures is the point in time when a teenager is considered an adult or is expected to accept adult responsibilities. In the United States, becoming eighteen years old or graduating from high school is usually considered the first major step to living independently as an adult. Becoming eighteen years old permits a person to vote in local and national elections, to drive a car, and, in some states, to buy alcoholic beverages.

Although many rites of passage happen because of the age of a person or dates on a calendar, most rites of passage are really journeys of self-discovery. Even though a teacher, a family member, or a friend may lead and assist us during the time from being a teenager to an adult, it is the individual's responsibility to learn and understand the lessons necessary for the next step in the journey of one's life.

$\mathcal{A}$bout You

Are there any customs or turning points in your own culture that are rites of passage from youth to adulthood? If so, what are they? Are there different customs for males and females? Have you participated in any particular rites of passage in your culture?

What are your own thoughts about the importance of rites of passage in a person's life? Do you agree that they are a necessary part of a person's journey toward self-discovery? Discuss these ideas with your partner or group.

$\mathcal{V}$ocabulary Preview Through Context Clues

Before listening to the next story, it will be helpful to preview some of the vocabulary you will hear. Previewing unfamiliar vocabulary words and idioms before listening can improve your general comprehension of the story and the events in it.

The sentences below contain the new vocabulary words and phrases in this chapter's essay. Read the sentences carefully and try to figure out the meanings by using context clues. Write your ideas on the line below each sentence.

1. The architect of that famous monument designed the building from his mental vision of it.

   I think that a *vision* is _____

   _____.

2. Some of the world-famous churches (cathedrals) in Europe were built during the 15th and 16th centuries.

   I think that a *cathedral* is _____

   _____.

3. The science-fiction movies in the Star Wars Trilogy are popular because they contain exciting stories about space travel.

   I think the *the Star Wars Trilogy* is _____

   _____.

4. Driver's Training, the name of the training course in many high schools where students learn how to drive a car, is popular with all the students.

   I think that *Driver's Training* is _____

   _____.

5. They couldn't believe all the magnificent scenery on the trip, like shining lakes, high mountains with snow, and beautiful ancient forests.

   I think that *magnificent* means _____

   _____.

6. Karen was not married, and it was presumptuous of Joe to think that she was already married just because she was 30 years old.

   I think that *presumptuous* means _____

   _____.

7. The computer school was always full because its branches were conveniently located at several different sites in the city.

I think that a *site* is _____

_____ .

8. The Indians had many interesting rituals in their New Year's celebration, such as saying several prayers and singing special songs.

I think that a *ritual* is _____

_____ .

9. Each edifice built in the city had to be designed with a strong structure because earthquakes were a danger there.

I think that an *edifice* is _____

_____ .

10. When any of the villagers had a problem or was sick, he or she visited the shaman, the person who cured illness or offered advice about a problem.

I think that a *shaman* is _____

_____ .

11. Many cultures have ceremonies that celebrate rites of passage from one period of life into another period, like weddings and children's births.

I think that a *rite of passage* is _____

_____ .

12. Students described Mr. Perry as "a truly maximum dude" because they liked him and respected him.

I think that *a truly maximum dude* is _____

_____ .

Vocabulary Quick-Check Review

Check your understanding of the new vocabulary words and phrases introduced in this chapter by completing the following matching exercise. Write the letter of the definition in Column B that matches the word or phrase in Column A.

Column A	Column B
1. _____ Star Wars	a. a course teaching how to drive
2. _____ presumptuous	b. a village healer
3. _____ shaman	c. custom
4. _____ ritual	d. place
5. _____ vision	e. describes someone who automatically thinks something or supposes something
6. _____ cathedral	f. mental picture
7. _____ Driver's Training	g. good guy
8. _____ site	h. beautiful
9. _____ rite of passage	i. custom that celebrates going from one part of life to another
10. _____ "truly maximum dude"	j. science-fiction movie
11. _____ magnificent	k. church
12. _____ edifice	l. building

*E*ssay Preview

Have you ever learned how to drive a car or how to operate any kind of machinery? Learning to drive a car in the United States is a rite of passage for teenagers. The skills needed to drive a car can greatly influence your personal life in many ways.

In this essay Fulghum tells the story of a drive he took with the high school driving teacher. At first, the work of teaching students how to drive seemed unimportant to Fulghum. But after listening to the teacher discuss his philosophy of driver's training, Fulghum understood the importance of driver education and why the students called the driving teacher "Master."

Why do you think the driving teacher was called "Master"?

*F*ocused Listening

Part 1

Look over the questions in each listening section before you listen to the tape. The questions will give you a general idea about the information contained in the essay. In addition, it will help you focus on the specific information needed to choose the best answer.

The listening exercises are divided into sections. The title of the chapter and the beginning of each listening section are announced by a speaker on the tape. Listen carefully and circle the best answer for each question.

When you've completed listening to Part 1, check your answers on the blackboard together as a whole class. If you wish, you may replay the complete tape—or just specific sections of it.

SECTION I

1. When Mr. Fulghum says the job of driver trainer is a job that any one with half a brain can do, he means
   a. it's an easy job.
   b. it's a hard job.
   c. everyone wants the job.

2. Fulghum said it would be an honor to teach a class in Driver's Training now that
   a. he sees it like Mr. Perry.
   b. he is a driving master.
   c. he's learned how to drive.

3. Students call Mr. Perry
   a. "the teaching master."
   b. "the driving master."
   c. "the gymnasium master."

4. The name Obi Wan Kenobi, the Wise One, comes from
   a. the *Wizard of Oz* movie.
   b. the movie *Gone with the Wind*.
   c. the Star Wars Trilogy movies.

SECTION II

5. Mr. Fulghum tells Mr. Perry,
   a. "I'd like to know how to drive a car."
   b. "I'd like to know if you like your job."
   c. "I'd like to know what you really do."

6. The Driver's Training students called Mr. Perry
   a. a "truly maximum dude."
   b. a "way-out guy."
   c. "grody to the max."

7. Mr. Perry tells Mr. Fulghum that he thinks of himself as
   a. a doctor.
   b. a shaman.
   c. a lawyer.

8. Mr. Perry thinks that he helps students
   a. write better.
   b. think about the past.
   c. think about this time in their lives.

9. Mr. Perry says we don't have any cultural rituals
   a. to acknowledge growing up.
   b. to acknowledge getting married.
   c. to acknowledge going to school.

10. Mr. Perry thinks driving a car is a rite of passage because
    a. it is a time when teenagers become adults.
    b. it's a lot of movement.
    c. it's fun.

11. Moving from the back seat to the front seat means
    a. you get a license.
    b. you get a ticket.
    c. you get power.

SECTION III

12. Mr. Perry says the students talk to him about
    a. dreams, hopes, and fears.
    b. how to get into college.
    c. how to buy a good car.

13. Mr. Perry says the students think he is "safe" to talk to because
    a. he was in the Navy.
    b. he doesn't see them often.
    c. he's a teacher.

14. Students ask Mr. Perry
    a. what it was like when he was young.
    b. what it was like to drive a bus.
    c. what it was like one hundred years ago.

15. Mr. Fulghum said his driving was improved along with his sense
    of place and
    a. address.
    b. purpose.
    c. phone number.

SECTION IV

16. Mr. Fulghum said that people came to Chartres to
    a. see the river.
    b. see the great church being built there.
    c. see the museum.

17. In the story, the first man the traveler spoke to was a stonemason
    who
    a. lifted rocks.
    b. dug up rocks.
    c. carved rocks.

18. The second man made slabs of glass because he was
    a. a painter.
    b. a glassblower.
    c. building his own house.

19. The third man was
    a. a blacksmith.
    b. a teacher.
    c. a priest.

20. The woman sweeping the work area said she was
    a. cleaning up the mess.
    b. there to help tourists.
    c. building a cathedral for the glory of "Almighty God."

SECTION V

21. Fulghum often thinks about the people of Chartres because
    a. they worked for something higher than themselves.
    b. they were such friendly people.
    c. they were doing such a great construction job.

22. The people in this story knew that they
    a. would not live to see their work completed.
    b. would live to see their work completed.
    c. would never die.

23. Fulghum thinks that Mr. Perry and the woman at Chartres are similar because
    a. they look alike.
    b. they both drive cars very well.
    c. they each followed a vision of how the world ought to be.

Part 2

In this listening section, you will listen to the complete essay again, but this time there will be no pauses or narration in between each section.

The sentences below contain information about the essay you just heard. In every sentence, there is some information about the essay which is not true. The information which is not true is <u>underlined</u>. The sentences are listed in the order that the information is heard on the tape. As you listen to the essay again, cross out the incorrect information and write the correct information below it.

1. Fulghum thinks that <u>many</u> teachers want to teach Driver's Training.

_____.

2. The students call Mr. Perry—who is their Driver's Training teacher—the "Driving Wizard."

_____.

3. Mr. Perry told Fulghum that he helps students move through the streets.

_____.

4. Mr. Perry says that having a driver's license is not important to his students.

_____.

5. Mr. Perry says that he rarely has conversations with his students while they are driving.

_____.

6. In the story about the cathedral in Chartres, France, the traveler meets a stonemason and an architect.

_____.

7. The woman who is leaning on her broom in this story tells the man that she is building a cathedral for money.

_____.

8. Fulghum says that Mr. Perry is not like the woman in the story about the cathedral in Chartres.

_____.

Listen to the tape again and then check your answers with the rest of the class.

*W*hat Do You Think?

Discuss with your class the answers to the following questions.

1. What impressions did you have about "old Mr. Perry"? Do you think you would enjoy meeting him? Why or why not?

2. What does Mr. Perry mean when he says that the students like him because he is "safe"?

3. What does Fulghum mean when he says that Mr. Perry and the lady sweeping the cathedral "share a vision of something higher than themselves"? Have you met any people with a similar "vision"? If yes, who were they?

4. What rites of passage in your culture did you participate in or share with other people? In what ways were you influenced by these events in your personal life? Do you think these "turning points" or "markers" are an important part of our life? Why or why not?

*C*lass Activity

Fulghum noted that Mr. Perry taught the students "both to drive a car and drive a life." Make a list of the ways driving a car and living a life are similar. Work with a partner. Here are two examples to start your list.

Driving a car	Living a life
Ex.: Learn to focus attention on the road.	Learn to focus attention on daily activities.
Ex.: Follow traffic signals.	Learn when to "go" and learn when to "stop."

1. _____   _____

   _____   _____

2. _____   _____

   _____   _____

3. _____   _____

   _____   _____

4. _____ _____

  _____ _____

5. _____ _____

  _____ _____

$\mathcal{R}$eflections: A Cross-Cultural Issue for Discussion or Composition

Fulghum thinks the students who have Mr. Perry will always remember him and what they learn from him. In a way, Mr. Perry's philosophy of teaching followed this model: "A good teacher is the guide on the side, not the sage* on the stage."

Mr. Perry thought he could help his students by showing them the direction they could learn best by themselves. Also, he never forced his own ideas on them; instead, he let them find out things by themselves.

Think about one of your teachers or another person in your life whose lessons you will always remember. What lessons did you learn from him or her? How have these lessons influenced your life? Does this person remind you of Mr. Perry in any way? Why or why not?

Prepare an oral presentation to share with your class about your experiences or write a composition on the same subject.

$\mathcal{D}$ictation

Listen and fill in the missing words.

I've often thought about the _____ of Chartres. They _____ some-

thing they knew they would never see _____. They built for

something _____ than themselves. They had a magnificent

_____.

*Sage —a smart, wise person

And for Jack Perry, it is the _____. He will never see his students

_____ _____. Few teachers _____. But from where he is and with what

he has, he _____ a vision of how the world _____ to be.

That old woman of Chartres was a _____ ancestor of the man

who teaches _____ _____, who is _____ a cathedral to

the _____ enterprise in his own _____ way. From him the kids

learn both to _____ a car and drive a _____—with _____.

*L*anguage of Culture: Hesitating

When you begin to learn a new language, it is often difficult to think
quickly of how to answer questions people ask you. A useful technique
in these situations is called "hesitating"—using specific words or phrases
to allow you to pause before answering a question. A few common "hesitating" words or phrases are :

So . . .	Uh . . .
Well . . .	Um . . .
Oh . . .	Gee . . .
I think . . .	I guess . . .
Let's see . . .	Ah . . .

Here are two examples from the Driver's Training essay.

1. When Fulghum began his conversation with Mr. Perry, he said: "So
   you're the man who teaches Driver Training." Mr. Perry paused to
   think of a way to answer by saying: "Well, that's my job title, yes."

2. Later on, Fulghum asked Perry: "But what about actually
   learning to operate a vehicle?" Perry hesitated and said, "Oh, that
   comes easily enough."

$\mathcal{P}$ractice 1

With a partner, practice the "hesitating" words or phrases below. Student A asks the question. Student B answers the question using a "hesitating" word or phrase at the beginning of the sentence.

Examples: Student A: Why did you come to the United States?
Student B: Gee, that's really a long story.
Student A: What did you think about today's English class?
Student B: Well, it was okay, but not great.

1. Student A: What do you think of the weather in this city?

    Student B: _____, _____

    _____.

2. Student A: How do you like American food?

    Student B: _____, _____

    _____.

3. Student A: Are you following the presidential election campaign?

    Student B: _____, _____

    _____.

4. Student A: If you could live anywhere in the world, where would you live?

    Student B: _____, _____

    _____.

5. Student A: What's your favorite free-time activity?

    Student B: _____, _____

    _____.

$\mathcal{P}$ractice 2

Write five questions of your own and have your partner answer them using a "hesitating" word or phrase.

1. Student A: _____?
   Student B: _____, _____
   _____.

2. Student A: _____?
   Student B: _____, _____
   _____.

3. Student A: _____?
   Student B: _____, _____
   _____.

4. Student A: _____?
   Student B: _____, _____
   _____.

5. Student A: _____?
   Student B: _____, _____
   _____.

"The Universe is change; our life is what our thoughts make it."
—*Marcus Antoninus*

Chapter 5

PERSONAL PERCEPTION

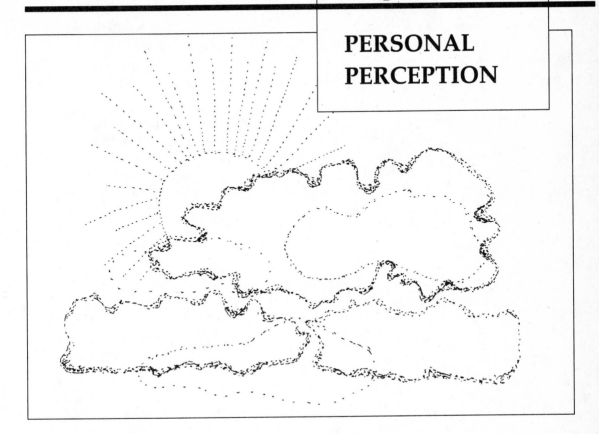

*T*here are many ways to interpret reality. Although several people may look at the same picture at the same time, they may interpret the same picture quite differently. Reality is created by our experiences, culture, and personalities. This experience of our very personal view of reality is called "perception."

Look carefully at the illustration on this page.

- What do you see happening in the picture?
- Does your "perception" change if you look at the picture from different angles?
- What clues do you see in the picture about the story in this chapter?

Share your results with the class.

$\mathcal{A}$bout Perception

Have you ever seen a movie or show with a friend or family member and found out that both of you had very different interpretations about the events and the meaning of the events you had just seen together? Or have you ever noticed that one person's favorite food is another person's most disliked food?

These varieties of personal experiences and interpretations are examples of personal perception (your own particular expression and interpretation of reality). In a way, our personal perceptions actually create what we think is real and true. For example, when a cat sees a bird, he perceives the bird as a very tasty and delicious meal! Yet a person viewing the same bird might see the bird as a wonderful singer or a very beautiful part of nature—and certainly not to be eaten.

In his book *Unconditional Life*, Deepak Chopra has a wonderful story that illustrates this point. A British anthropologist (a scientist who studies the culture and behavior of different peoples) was visiting and observing a group of people living in the forests of India. One night, while the anthropologist was quietly walking in the forest, he saw an Indian holy man dancing joyfully. The holy man was embracing trees, laughing when he heard the sound of the wind in the leaves, and smiling in the moonlight. There were no other people around.

Feeling very shocked at this man's strange, solitary behavior,* the anthropologist went to the holy man and asked him why he was dancing alone in the forest. The holy man looked surprised and answered: "What makes you think that I am alone?"

The perception of the holy man was that he was surrounded in the forest by natural spirits, and this gave him great joy and happiness. He did not perceive that he was alone. The anthropologist, however, did not perceive spirits in the forest. Can we say which perception, that of the holy man or that of the anthropologist, was correct and which was incorrect? Do you think they could both be correct?

*Solitary behavior—behavior of someone who is alone.

$\mathcal{A}$bout You

Can you remember any experiences in your life when a friend or family member perceived a situation in a completely different way than you did? For example, was there ever a time when you tried to advise or warn someone about trouble you could see but he or she could not see? Did this person follow your advice? Why do you think you both had such different ideas about the same situation? Were there differences in culture? Differences in past experiences? Do you think you would both perceive that situation today as you did in the past? Why or why not?

Describe this experience in your life to your partner. Then make a list with your partner of all the things you both can think of that create a perception of things, such as culture and language.

$\mathcal{V}$ocabulary Preview Through Context Clues

Before listening to the next story, it will be helpful to preview some of the vocabulary you will hear. Previewing unfamiliar vocabulary words and idioms before listening can improve your general comprehension of the story and the events in it.

The sentences below contain the new vocabulary words and phrases in this chapter's essay. Read the sentences carefully and try to figure out the meanings of the unfamiliar words by using context clues. Fill in the line below each sentence with the meaning of the italicized word or phrase.

1. Mark is usually inclined to vote Republican, but this year he surprisingly voted for a Democrat.

   I think that *inclined to* means _____

   _____.

2. The quarterback and tight end, two players on a football team, are very important for the team's success.

   I think that *the quarterback and tight end* are _____

   _____.

3. Because many buildings in which people worked were destroyed during the earthquake, the earthquake had a big impact on the San Francisco economy.

I think that *an impact* means _____

_____.

4. Roberta said, "Oooo-wow!" because she was so excited when she saw my beautiful new car.

I think that *"Oooo-wow!"* means _____

_____.

5. I didn't do last night's homework, so if the teacher asks me a question about it, I'll just die! (feel very embarrassed and upset)

I think that *"I'll just die"* means _____

_____.

6. It's often hard for Betty to cope with all her responsibilities because she works full time and takes care of the house and three children by herself.

I think that *to cope* means _____

_____.

7. God is sometimes called "the Mystery of Mysteries" because many people think God is mysterious.

I think that *"the Mystery of Mysteries "* is _____

_____.

8. The librarian was happy to report that the signature under Lincoln's picture really was Lincoln's bona fide (true) signature.

I think that *bona fide* means _____

_____.

9. Kids love to take a lump of clay and create figures of people and things from it.

I think that *a lump* is _____

_____.

10. He wants all the available information about how this planet evolved because he is interested in how this planet developed.

I think that *evolved* means _____

11. Mike tossed the basketball to his teammate Bruce because Bruce was very close to the basket.

I think that *toss* means _____

_____.

12. It was only a small problem, but he acted like it was a monumental problem.

I think that *monumental* means _____

_____.

13. All laboratory people must be rubber-gloved because gloves protect them at all times.

I think that *rubber-gloved* means _____

_____.

14. Projection (thinking that other people will act and think the way we do) influences our opinion.

I think that *projection* means _____

_____.

$\mathcal{V}$ocabulary Quick-Check Review

Check your understanding of the new words and phrases introduced in this chapter by completing the following matching exercise. Write the letter of the definition in Column B that matches the word or phrase on Column A.

Column A

1. _____ quarterback and tight end
2. _____ a lump
3. _____ evolve
4. _____ "oooo-wow"

5. _____ bona fide
6. _____ a projection

7. _____ "I'll just die"
8. _____ to be inclined
9. _____ "Mystery of Mysteries"
10. _____ monumental

11. _____ an impact

12. _____ rubber-gloved
13. _____ cope
14. _____ toss

Column B

a. be able to do it
b. describes something real
c. preferring one way to do things
d. thinking that other people would act and think the same way you act and think

e. words of excitement
f. move from one step to another

g. big
h. players in football
i. the creator of the world
j. something without an exact shape

k. an influence and effect on something

l. throw
m. wearing rubber gloves
n. phrase showing nervousness about having to do something

$\mathcal{E}$ssay Preview

"Personal Perception" begins in a high school drawing class. Mr. Fulghum, the art teacher, is teaching a lesson about the internal anatomy of the human brain. At first he uses a cantaloupe (a type of fruit) to demonstrate the true size and shape of a brain. Later, a student brings in a real brain from her father's scientific laboratory.

Although the class lesson began about anatomy (the study of the external and internal form of the body), it concludes with messages about human perception and current brain research. Fulghum describes fascinating findings about recent brain research. In fact, this new information actually changes the way he thinks about getting along with other people.

Do you have any ideas about what this new information might be?

$\mathcal{F}$ocused Listening

Part 1

Look over the questions in each listening section before you listen to the tape. The questions will give you a general idea about the information contained in the essay. In addition, it will help you focus on the specific information needed to choose the best answer.

The listening exercises are divided into sections. The titles of the chapter and the beginning of each listening section are announced by a speaker on the tape. Listen carefully and circle the best answer for each question.

When you've completed listening to Part 1, check your answers on the blackboard together as a whole class. If you wish, you may replay the complete tape—or just specific sections of it.

SECTION I

1. When the teacher begins the class, he is thinking
   a. about the football game.
   b. he can't believe he's doing this.
   c. he wants to see a movie.

2. He reached into a white plastic bag and pulled out
   a. a rabbit.
   b. a monkey brain.
   c. a human brain.

3. When the students think that if he hands them the brain they "will die," they mean
   a. they will feel embarrassed and scared.
   b. they will really die.
   c. they will laugh.

4. When the brain is given back to the teacher, he
   a. tosses it on the basketball court.
   b. tosses it to the quarterback of the football team.
   c. tosses it in the trash can.

5. When the tight end drops the brain,
   a. he cries.
   b. it bounces.
   c. it breaks.

SECTION II

6. Fulghum was using the brain in a beginning
   a. drawing class.
   b. biology class.
   c. chemistry class.

7. He had been lecturing on
   a. sound research.
   b. color research.
   c. brain research.

8. When Fulghum previously used a cantaloupe as a model of a brain, the students thought the lesson was
   a. boring.
   b. very interesting.
   c. only for kids.

9. Fulghum's student was able to bring a real brain to school because her father
   a. collected brains at home.
   b. built models of brains.
   c. was a neurosurgeon at a research laboratory.

10. When Fulghum shouted to his students, "Bring a brain to school—all of you," he meant
    a. everyone should get his own brain from the laboratory.
    b. everyone should come to class ready to use his or her brain to learn.
    c. everyone should go meet the brain neurosurgeon.

SECTION III

11. Fulghum says the students thought seeing the real brain was an "oooo-wow" experience because
    a. it seemed amazing.
    b. it seemed very boring.
    c. it was shaped like a cantaloupe.

12. Fulghum says his brain meat was fueled by
    a. yesterday's baloney sandwich, corn chips, and a coke.
    b. yesterday's baloney sandwich, fries, and coffee.
    c. yesterday's baloney sandwich, potato chips, and milk.

13. Fulghum says he can understand the mechanical working of the brain because it is like
    a. a computer.
    b. an air conditioner.
    c. a motor.

SECTION IV

14. Fulghum includes the following things in his brain contents:
    a. the face of his wife when he was young and the cry of his first-born son.
    b. how to cook a chicken and how to sing.
    c. a Picasso painting and his junior high teachers.

15. Fulghum says that the brain contains
    a. 10 billion suns.
    b. 10 billion bits of information.
    c. 10 billion planets.

SECTION V

16. The most important fact to come out of brain research is
    a. we are different on the outside but the same on the inside.
    b. we are as different on the outside as we are on the inside.
    c. we are the same on the inside and the same on the outside.

17. Fulghum says the way each person sees things is
    a. a projection from his or her own mind.
    b. always the same as others.
    c. easy to predict.

18. Because each person's brain is so different, Fulghum is surprised that
    a. we can see each other.
    b. we can hear each other.
    c. we can communicate with each other.

SECTION VI

19. From a practical point of view, this information makes Fulghum
    a. less patient with the people he lives with.
    b. more patient with the people he lives with.
    c. very confused.

20. Fulghum now has more patience with other people's opinions because
    a. it makes his wife happier.
    b. he is a minister.
    c. he recognizes how differently all of our brains work.

21. Instead of asking people "Why don't you see it the way I do?," he now says,
    a. "You see it that way? How amazing?"
    b. "You see it that way? How amazing!"
    c. "You see it that way? That's stupid!"

SECTION VII

22. Fulghum reports that Einstein's brain is now in a lab jar
    a. in Fulghum's home.
    b. on the moon.
    c. in Missouri.

23. When scientists studied Einstein's real brain in the laboratory, they found out that
    a. his brain was just like everyone's.
    b. his brain was different from the brains of other people.
    c. they couldn't reach a conclusion.

24. When a guest once asked Einstein to show him his laboratory, he pointed to his own head because
    a. his laboratory was really his own brain.
    b. he was having a terrible headache.
    c. he didn't understand the question.

25. Fulghum calls Einstein pointing to his head an "oooo-wow" experience because
    a. he suddenly understood that Einstein's brain was part of "the Mystery of Mysteries," too.
    b. his students wanted to study Einstein's brain.
    c. other scientists had already studied Einstein's brain.

Part 2

In this listening section, you will listen to the complete essay again, but this time there will be no pauses or narration in between each section.

The sentences below contain information about the essay you just heard. In every sentence, there is some information about the essay which is not true. The information which is not true is underlined. The sentences are listed in the order that the information is heard on the tape. As you listen to the essay again, cross out the incorrect information and write the correct information below it.

1. The teacher feels very underlined comfortable when he pulls a human brain out of a plastic bag.

    _____.

2. All the students hope that the teacher will give them the brain to hold.

    _____.

3. Fulghum brought the brain to his English class.

    _____.

4. Before they had used a real brain, they had tossed around a <u>basketball</u>.

   _____.

5. One student brought a real brain to class because his <u>mother</u> worked in a laboratory.

   _____.

6. When the students asked Fulghum what he thought about the real brain, he began to describe his ideas about <u>driving a truck</u>.

   _____.

7. Fulghum compared the brain to a <u>bicycle</u>.

   _____.

8. Fulghum says that new research on the human brain shows that the inside of each person's head is <u>the same as every other</u> person's head.

   _____.

9. Fulghum says that every person has <u>the same</u> perception of reality.

   _____.

10. Fulghum says he has <u>less patience</u> with his family now that he knows more about our brains.

    _____.

   Listen to the tape again and check your answers with the rest of the class.

*W*hat Do You Think?

1. Were you surprised that Fulghum used a real brain in the classroom? Why or why not?

2. Fulghum describes the "oooo-wow " experience as a moment when you suddenly understand something that confused you before. Can you remember an experience in your life when you also had this sudden moment of understanding? Tell your story to the group.

3. Now that you have heard this essay, how would you answer the question "What is reality?"? What have you learned about the recent results of human brain research? Do you think this information will influence your thinking about people in any way? If yes, in what way?

*C*lass Activity

Fulghum lists the large variety of memories that are in his personal "brain meat," such as the fifty years of dreams and a recipe for how to cook a turkey. Make a list of some of your favorite "brain meat" memories and share the list with your group or class. Include such things as memories of special people, foods you like or hate, and so on. Here are two examples to start your list:

1. Childhood memories at home in my country.

2. How to cook tamales.

3. _____ .

4. _____ .

5. _____ .

Share your answers with the rest of the class.

$\mathcal{R}$eflections: A Cross-Cultural Issue for Discussion or Composition

"First impressions are lasting ones."

"First impressions" are the ideas or perceptions we develop about something or someone we meet or see for the first time. These impressions can be very important and can be the beginning of our future opinions about that person or thing. Sometimes we later realize that our first impressions were really incorrect and we then have to change our original impressions.

Can you remember a time in your life when your first impressions about someone or something were correct? Can you recall an experience when you had to change your first impressions about something or someone close to you? Prepare an oral presentation to share with your class about your experiences or write a composition on the same subject.

$\mathcal{D}$ictation

Listen and fill in the missing words.

The single most _____ statement to come out of _____ research

in the last twenty-five years is this: We are as _____ from one

another on the _____ of our heads as we appear to be different from

one another on the _____ of our heads.

Look around and see the infinite variety of human _____ — skin, hair,

_____, ethnic characteristics, size, color, _____. And know that on

the inside such differences are even greater—what we know, how we

_____, how we process _____, what we remember and forget,

our strategies for functioning and coping. _____ to that the under-

standing the "world" out "there" is as much a _____ from

inside our heads as it is a _____, and pretty soon you are up against the realization that it is a miracle that we _____ at all. It

is almost _____ that we are dealing with the same

_____.

Language of Culture: Different Ways to Call People

Ways of addressing people – calling them by name or title – are different in every culture. Many new American immigrants and visitors to the United States express great surprise at the informal* way Americans address each other.

An example of this informality can be seen in the "Eyes of the Beholder" essay. Notice in the essay's last paragraph the informal way Fulghum refers to the honored and world-famous scientist Albert Einstein. Fulghum begins, "When Big Al was in residence at the Institute for Advanced Studies at Princeton . . . " Giving Einstein the nickname "Big Al" may be considered disrespectful in many cultures, but Fulghum knows that most Americans reading his essay will realize the author not only highly respects this great scientist but also cares deeply about Einstein.

Recognizing that forms of address are generally, but not always, informal in the United States can help you understand a main part of American culture. You will also understand American culture better if you keep in mind the following information.

1. Most Americans have at least two names – their first name, chosen by parents at birth, and their last name, carried down from generation to generation usually by the husband's family. For example, an American whose name is Roger Aldridge has been given his first name by his parents and has inherited** his last name from his father.

    Until recently, an American woman would use her family name as her last name before she married. After marriage she would drop her family name (the last name of her father) and take her husband's family name. For example, Joan Villard is a single woman. Her first name is Joan; her last name is Villard. If she married a man named Benjamin Whitely, her name would become Joan Whitely. More and

*Informal—casual.
**Inherited—something you get when you are born.

more, however, an American woman marrying today chooses to keep her original family name or add it to her new husband's name. For example, when Joan Whitely marries Benjamin Villard, she might choose to call herself Joan Villard-Whitely, Joan Whitely, or remain Joan Villard.

2. The formal written and/or spoken way to address men and women in the United States is to precede the name with the following abbreviated forms: "Mr." for married and single men; "Ms." for married and single women; "Miss" for single women; and "Mrs." for married women. (Pronunciation: Mr. = Mister; Ms. = Miz; Mrs. = Missus) For example, Roger Aldridge becomes Mr. Aldridge, and Joan Villard becomes Miss Villard, Mrs. Villard-Whitely, or Mrs. Whitely.

3. On the job, a new worker is often introduced to his or her supervisor using "Mr." or "Ms." in front of the last name. After a few minutes or a few days, however, the supervisor may ask the worker to call him or her by his or her first name. If one is not sure what name to use, one should use "Mr." or "Ms." and the person's last name. Co-workers are called by their first name.

Here's an example.

Today is Juan's first day in the company. His co-worker, Martin, is introducing him to other workers.

Juan:	Martin, I'd like to introduce you to Marina. She'll be helping you with the accounting.
Martin:	Hello, Marina. Nice to meet you.
Juan:	Let's walk over to Joe's office. He's the supervisor of this department.
Martin:	Joe?
Juan:	Yes. Joe Sullivan.
Martin:	Oh. The supervisor?
Juan:	Sure. Here he is. Joe, here's Martin, our new desk clerk.

Joe:	Nice to meet you, Martin. (Martin is not sure what to do. Juan called the supervisor "Joe," but it's Martin's first meeting with him. What should he do?)
Martin:	Um . . . uh . . . Hello, Mr. Sullivan. I'm very happy to meet you. (Martin wasn't sure what to call Joe since it was his first meeting with him, so he correctly chose a formal way, using "Mr." in front of the last name.)
Joe:	Oh, you can call me Joe!
Martin:	Oh, thanks, Joe. (Juan takes Martin back to his desk.)

Note: When you're not sure what to call someone, ask: "What would you like me to call you?"

Practice this dialogue orally in groups of three.

TRUE OR FALSE STATEMENTS

Answer the following True or False statements. Write "True" on the line below the statement if the sentence is true. If the sentence is false, write "False" on the line and, on the line below, explain why the sentence is false.

1. In general, forms of addressing people are very informal in the United States.

   _____

   _____.

2. Americans usually call each other by their last names at home or at work.

   _____

   _____.

3. Americans usually get their last name or family name from their father.

   _____

   _____.

4. It's usually okay to call your boss by his or her first name the first time you meet him or her.

   _____

   _____.

5. You can use the title "Ms" for married or single women.

   _____

   _____.

6. The title "Miss" is used only for married women.

   _____

   _____.

> *"There are two ways of spreading light:*
> *To be the candle, or the mirror which*
> *reflects it."*
>
> —*Edith Wharton*

Chapter 6

LIGHT
REFLECTIONS

$\mathcal{L}$ight, both direct and reflected, plays an important part in our impressions about people and life around us. Reflected light, images created when light bends back from its original surface, is most commonly seen in mirrors and photographs. In both examples, direct light was reversed and created a new impression or product.

The illustration on this page shows the reflection of a woman in a mirror.

- What impressions do you get about her mood, her feelings, and her personality?
- Do you think you would have the same impressions if you looked directly at the woman's face instead of at the reflection?
  Why or why not?

- Now look at the quotation above the picture. In what ways are the light of a candle and the light reflected from the candle the same and in what ways are they different?
- What are your ideas about a person "reflecting" light?

Discuss these ideas with a partner.

About Reflections and Light

When we think about reflections, the ideas of light (from the sun or artificially made) and dark (shadows, shade, night) often come to our mind. The English language has many words and phrases about the relationship of light to darkness. "Light" is most often used to express something positive, good, or truthful. We call people with special wisdom "enlightened" (having the light). A happy person or someone in a good mood is called "lighthearted."

Darkness is seen as the opposite of light. It is used to express something negative, mysterious, or unknown. In politics, we call a person who is not expected to win an election a "dark horse." If someone has a very difficult emotional experience, we may say that that person is passing through the "heart of darkness."

An interrelationship of light and darkness is very beautifully expressed in Genesis, the first book of the Bible: "And God said, 'Let there be light,' and there was light. And God saw the light that it was good, and God divided the light from the darkness."

About You

In what ways are light and darkness described and written about in your culture? Is it similar or different from how it is described in American culture?

Take a look at these additional popular English idioms using "light" and "dark." Try to guess their meaning with a partner.

1. The doctors and Bill's family kept him in the dark about his disease.

2. The workers didn't understand the new rules, so they asked their supervisor to shed some light on them.

3. Joe's friends all knew he was making a mistake, but they waited for him to see the light himself.

List a few idioms or phrases about light and darkness from your own language and culture below. Share them with a partner or the class.

1. _____

2. _____

3. _____

$\mathcal{V}$ocabulary Preview Through Context Clues

Before listening to the story about light reflections, it will be helpful to preview some of the vocabulary you will hear. Previewing unfamiliar vocabulary words and idioms before listening can improve your general comprehension of the story and the events in it.

The sentences below contain the new vocabulary words and phrases you will hear in this chapter's essay. Read the sentences carefully and try to figure out their meanings by using context clues. Write your ideas on the line below each sentence.

1. A monastery, the building where monks live, is usually a very quiet place.

   I think that a *monastery* is _____

   _____.

2. Today a bitter residue of bad feelings is still left over because they were hated enemies during the war.

   I think that *residue* means _____

   _____.

3. After the German army marched into Russia, Russia bombed Germany in retribution because they wanted to punish Germany for invading Russia.

I think that *retribution* means _____

_____.

4. Because the heavy rainstorm made the roads inaccessible by car, they had to reach the village by helicopter.

I think that *inaccessible* means _____

_____.

5. Metaphors are language used to show a relationship of something similar between two things, such as Shakespeare's famous metaphor "All the world's a stage."

I think that a *metaphor* is _____

_____.

6. The glass broke into many fragments when it hit the floor because it was thin and very fragile.

I think that *fragments* are _____

_____.

7. We went to see Dr. Bonner because he has an excellent reputation as the best heart specialist in the country.

I think that *reputation* means _____

_____.

8. Most kids in the class hated to do homework, but Alma was an exception because she loved to do homework.

I think that an *exception* is _____

_____.

9. The library director needed to recruit (enroll) fifteen new volunteers for the summer Children's Reading Program.

I think that *to recruit* means _____

_____.

10. The soldiers made a night assault on the enemy because they wanted to surprise and kill them.

I think that an *assault* is _____

_____.

11. Most of the village people were poor peasants, farmers who worked on their own land.

I think that a *peasant* is _____

_____.

12. Mother Teresa is a living legend, a famous person who is alive, recognized, and admired by many people around the world.

I think that a *living legend* means _____

_____.

13. Although it seemed like a paradox to build a peace center at the site of a terrible war, it became a very successful school for change.

I think that a *paradox* is _____

_____.

14. The partisans, fighters from the villages, continued to fight the occupation of their land by foreign troops.

I think that the *partisans* are _____

_____.

15. The two opposing sides had a *rapprochement* and stopped fighting, but there was still a lot of hatred between them.

I think that a *"rapprochement"* means _____

_____.

$\mathcal{V}$ocabulary Quick-Check Review

Check your understanding of the new words and phrases introduced in this chapter by completing the following matching exercise. Write the letter of the definition in Column B that matches the word or phrase in Column A.

Column A	Column B
1. _____ monastery	a. a small piece from an object
2. _____ a living legend	b. a home or place for a religious group
3. _____ a fragment	c. agreement
4. _____ to recruit	d. fighters who defend their land
5. _____ retribution	e. to enroll
6. _____ peasant	f. an attack
7. _____ an assault	g. something describing a thing similar to another thing
8. _____ a paradox	h. a contradiction
9. _____ a reputation	i. something leftover
10. _____ inaccessible	j. what a person has if he is well-liked
11. _____ metaphor	k. a well-known and admired person
12. _____ an exception	l. something not like the others
13. _____ partisans	m. not able to be reached
14. _____ residue	n. describes the action of getting even with somebody
15. _____ rapprochement	o. village person who works on a farm

*E*ssay Preview

One summer Fulghum attended an institute in order to study about Greek culture and philosophy. The institute was in Gonia, a town on the island of Crete. During World War II, on this exact site, the villagers of Gonia fought against the German troops who invaded the island. The villagers had no military weapons but fought with great courage. Leftover from the war was a great hatred between the Cretans and the Germans who occupied the island.

Today in this place there is an institute dedicated to peace among all people, and the institute's director is a man whom Fulghum greatly admires. While Fulghum was at the institute, he learned an important lesson that has deeply affected his own philosophy of life.

What kind of lesson do you think Fulghum learned?

*F*ocused Listening

Part 1

Look over the questions in each listening section before you listen to the tape. The questions will give you a general idea about the information contained in the essay. In addition, it will help you focus on the specific information needed to choose the best answer.

The listening exercises are divided into sections. The titles of the chapter and the beginning of each listening section are announced by a speaker on the tape. Listen carefully and circle the best answer for each question.

When you've completed listening to Part 1, check your answers on the blackboard together as a whole class. If you wish, you may replay the complete tape—or just specific sections of it.

SECTION I

1. Usually, when speakers finish their talk, they turn to the audience and ask:
   a. Are you happy you came?
   b. Would you like to leave now?
   c. Are there any questions?

2. The question Fulghum likes to ask is:
   a. What is the meaning of life?
   b. Where's the cafeteria?
   c. How do I get to the airport?

3. Fulghum says he got an answer to that question
   a. many times.
   b. only once.
   c. never.

SECTION II

4. The place of the story Fulghum tells is
   a. really in his imagination.
   b. on the island of Crete.
   c. in the United States.

5. The Greek monastery is in
   a. the capital of Greece.
   b. the village of Gonia.
   c. a different country.

6. Next to the monastery is
   a. an institute for understanding and peace.
   b. an institute to learn the techniques of war.
   c. an institute for engineers.

SECTION III

7. The site of the institute overlooks
   a. the ocean.
   b. a beautiful garden.
   c. the exact place the Nazis invaded the island and were attacked by the people of Crete.

8. From this site, a person can also see a cemetery
   a. for the Nazis.
   b. for both the Nazis and the Cretans.
   c. for the Cretans.

9. During World War II,
   a. Crete successfully defended itself against the Nazis.
   b. the Nazis took over Crete.
   c. Crete was not involved in the war.

10. The only weapon the Cretans had at the end was
    a. love.
    b. friendship.
    c. hate.

11. Fulghum says that putting a peace institute in the same place
    where there are terrible war memories is
    a. a bad idea.
    b. a crazy idea.
    c. a paradox.

SECTION IV

12. Christos Papaderos is
    a. a doctor of philosophy and a teacher.
    b. a medical doctor and a student.
    c. a singer and an entertainer.

13. Dr. Papaderos believed
    a. the Germans and the Cretans had a lot to learn from each other.
    b. the Germans and Cretans would never get along.
    c. people should forget everything that happened in the war.

14. Fulghum felt that Christos Papaderos was a man
    a. with great weaknesses.
    b. no one listens to.
    c. he will always remember.

15. Papaderos's dream of building a peace center
    a. never happened.
    b. came true.
    c. was ignored.

SECTION V

16. When Fulghum came to the institute, Papaderos was
    a. not his teacher.
    b. already a living legend.
    c. already gone.

17. Papaderos finished his speech, walked across the room, and said:
    a. "What is the meaning of life?"
    b. "Are there any questions?"
    c. "Everyone can go home now."

18. Fulghum asked Papaderos,
    a. "When were you born?"
    b. "Where's the cafeteria?"
    c. "What is the meaning of life?"

19. Papaderos took out his wallet and pulled out a mirror
    a. the size of a fist.
    b. the size of a small stone.
    c. the size of a quarter.

SECTION VI

20. Papaderos said he found the mirror in a place where
    a. a German motorcycle had been wrecked.
    b. a German car had been wrecked.
    c. a German village was destroyed.

21. He saw the mirror was in many pieces so he decided to
    a. throw it all away.
    b. keep the smallest piece.
    c. keep the biggest piece.

22. He made a game with the mirror to
    a. try to find the missing pieces.
    b. reflect light into dark places.
    c. make shadows with the sun.

23. As Papaderos got older, the mirror became a metaphor for what he believed was the meaning of life. He believed:
    a. The dark places of people's hearts can never change.
    b. There is no purpose to reflect light in the mirror.
    c. Light will shine into dark places of people's hearts if you reflect the light.

24. When Fulghum left the institute,
    a. he forgot the information about Greek culture but always remembered the mirror.
    b he remembered everything about Greek culture and remembered about the mirror too.
    c. he remembered everything about Greek culture and forgot about the mirror.

Part 2

In this listening section, you will listen to the complete essay again, but this time there will be no pauses or narration in between each section.

The sentences below contain information about the essay you just heard. In every sentence, there is some information about the essay which is not true. The information which is not true is <u>underlined</u>. The sentences are listed in the order that the information is heard on the tape. As you listen to the essay again, cross out the incorrect information and write the correct information below it.

1. When Fulghum goes to lectures and meetings, he often asks the question "What is the meaning of <u>baseball</u>?"

   _____.

2. Fulghum describes an institute dedicated to <u>war</u> on the island of Crete.

   _____.

3. This island has a history of <u>Russian</u> paratroopers and Cretans fighting each other.

   _____.

4. Christos Papaderos is a famous <u>medical</u> doctor.

   _____.

5. When Fulghum asks Papaderos the question about life's meaning, Papaderos <u>does not answer</u> him.

   _____.

6. Papaderos takes out a mirror from <u>a large box in the room</u>.

   _____.

7. Papaderos says the mirror reminds him to reflect <u>dark shadows onto light</u> places in the world.

_____.

8. Fulghum says he <u>doesn't remember anything</u> from his trip to Greece.

_____.

Listen to the essay again and check your answers with the rest of the class.

$\mathcal{W}$hat Do You Think?

Discuss with your class the answers to the following questions.

1. What happened during World War II in the same location as the monastery? Why did Papaderos choose this location for his peace studies center?

2. What was your opinion about about Mr. Papaderos's story and his description of the mirror? Did anything surprise you? If so, what? Is it an easy or difficult story to believe? Explain your answer.

3. What impressions did you have of Mr. Papaderos? What kind of person do you think he is? Describe him in your own words.

4. Fulghum calls Dr. Papaderos a "living legend," meaning he is a man known and honored by many people during his lifetime. Are there any people in your country's culture whom you would call a "living legend"? Who are they? What have they done?

5. The experiences of the Nazis and Cretans during World War II are similar to the experiences of other nations who are at war with one another. Some people think that war is a necessary part of human history. Other people think that war is not necessary and can be prevented. What opinion do you have about war? Explain your answer.

Class Activity

Mr. Papaderos describes the importance of the small mirror he found as a child. This mirror and the memories attached to it lifted his spirits whenever he had a problem in his life.

Think about your own life and the times you have had to make difficult decisions or face a difficult situation. Was there a person or an object that lifted your spirits? Describe this person or object.

Look at the following form. It is a sample from a personal journal, a notebook an individual writes in about his or her feelings and experiences in life. Pretend this is a page from your own personal journal. Fill in the information about the person or object that has helped you.

<u>My Journal</u>

August 12, 1993

Today I have been thinking about how important _____

is to me. _____ has been there to help me with so many

things I've done. First, I remember the time when _____

_____.

Then, I also remember the time when _____

_____.

When I think of the future, I feel confident that _____

will always be there to help me.

After you've filled in the journal form, share it with your partner.

$\mathcal{R}$eflections: A Cross-Cultural Issue for Discussion or Composition

It is common for countries to honor the memories of the people who died defending their country. The peace center created by Mr. Papaderos, which was located in a place with powerful memories of love and hate between different groups of people, is a good example of this.

It is also common for individuals to remember and honor their friends and family who died. This is done with different types of observances that occur in their homes, places of religion, and in their hearts.

What personal customs or ceremonies do you follow to honor and remember friends or family members who have died? What are some of the major historical events remembered and observed in your culture? How are they celebrated?

Prepare an oral presentation for the class about some of these observances in your culture, or write a composition about them to share with the class.

$\mathcal{D}$ictation

Listen and fill in the missing words.

When I was a child, during the war, we were very poor and we lived in a remote _____ . One day, on the road, I found the broken pieces of a _____ . A German motorcycle had been wrecked in that place.

I tried to find all the _____ and put them together, but it was not _____, so I kept only the _____ piece. This one. And by scratching it on a _____ I made it round. I began to play with it as a _____ became fascinated by the fact that I could reflect _____ into dark places where the sun would never shine—

into _____ holes and dark _____. It became a

_____ for me to get light into the most _____

places I could find.

I _____ the little mirror, and as I went about my growing up, I

would take it out in idle _____ and continue the challenge of

the game. As I became a man, I grew to _____ that this was

not just a child's game but a _____ for what I might do with

my life. I came to understand that I am not the _____ or the

_____ of light. But light—truth, understanding, knowledge—is

there, and it will only _____ in many _____ places if I

reflect it.

Language of Culture: Ways to Let People Know You Want to Speak

In conversation, every culture provides techniques to let someone in the
conversation know that you have something to say. We call these techniques "attention-focusing" because you are focusing attention on yourself as the next speaker.

Fulghum demonstrates one popular attention-focusing technique in this
story. Dr. Papaderos invited his audience to ask questions, and Fulghum
had a question to ask. Before he could ask his question, however, he
needed to focus Dr. Papaderos's attention on himself in a polite way so
that Dr. Papaderos would know that he had a question. The way
Fulghum did this was by stating Dr. Papaderos's name first (to focus
attention) and then by asking his question.

Dr. Papaderos: Are there any questions? No questions?
Fulghum: Dr. Papaderos (states name first), what is the
meaning of life? (asks question)

Here are a few more examples of this technique:

Dr. Brown, do you know when the patient can return home?

Judi, do you know what time it is?
Lucille, have you heard from your kids in New York yet?

Another common attention-focusing technique is to introduce your statement or question with one of the following phrases:

You know, . . .
In my opinion, . . .
Excuse me, . . .
By the way, . . .
It seems to me . . .

Examples:

You know, I'm not sure we should go to the movies tonight.
In my opinion, the book was very good.
Excuse me, are you the program director?
It seems to me we should take a vote of all the members.
By the way, have you met our new supervisor yet?

$\mathcal{P}$ractice 1

Complete the following sentences with a question or a statement.

1. Excuse me, _____?

2. It seems to me _____.

3. You know, _____.

4. By the way, _____?

5. In my opinion, _____.

*P*ractice 2

Have your partner complete the following sentences by using attention-focusing techniques.

Examples:

Student A: _____, did you see the news show on drugs last night?

Student B: <u>By the way</u>, did you see the news show on drugs last night?

Student A: _____, is this your first day at work?

Student B: Excuse me, is this your first day at work?

1. Student A: _____, do you know where the post office is?

   Student B: _____?

2. Student A: _____, the soccer team isn't doing so well this week.

   Student B: _____.

3. Student A: _____, I think it's time to leave.

   Student B: _____.

4. Student A: _____, I think it would be nice to go to a movie tonight.

   Student B: _____.

5. Student A: _____, the professor's talk was very boring.

   Student B: _____.

"Our life is frittered away [used up] by details."

—*Henry David Thoreau*

Chapter 7

THE STICK-POLISHING FANTASY

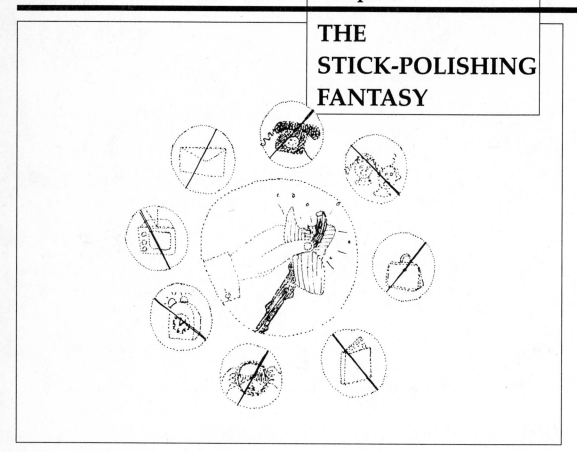

*H*ave you ever felt that too much of your time is spent on things you *must* do rather than on things you *like* to do? One way some people change these unpleasant jobs into pleasant jobs is to daydream while doing these things. When you daydream, you focus your mind on other topics and think about your own special dreams while you are awake.

The illustrations on this page show examples of what Americans idiomatically call "Things to Do"; these examples are seen in the circles surrounding the center circle of the illustrations on this page. The illustration in the center circle represents one man's daydream escape from everyday jobs.

- With a partner, make a list of the eight "things to do" shown in the small circles.
- Do you like or dislike the jobs illustrated in these pictures?
- The title of this chapter is a clue about the fantasy inside the center circle. What do you think this story is about?

About Being Organized

It has been suggested that there are two types of people: those who are organized and those who are disorganized. Organized people often know their daily schedules by heart. They are always on time, always know where to locate something, and always keep their houses neat and clean. Disorganized people, on the other hand, have great trouble remembering their daily schedule, even if they write it down. They frequently lose important things like house and car keys, schedule books, wallets, and documents. Their houses are often a mess. Not only do they often daydream *while* doing chores, they often daydream *instead* of doing chores!

About You

Which type are you? Do you think you are organized or disorganized? Explain your answer.

Do you think being an organized person is an important personal characteristic? Is being organized an important value in your culture? Why or why not? Discuss these questions and your answers with your partner.

Vocabulary Preview Through Context Clues

Before listening to the story about the stick-polishing fantasy, it will be helpful to preview some of the vocabulary you will hear in this chapter's essay. Previewing unfamiliar vocabulary words and idioms before listening to each chapter's essay can improve your general comprehension of the story and the events in it.

The sentences below contain the new vocabulary words and phrases. Read the sentences carefully and try to figure out the meanings of the new vocabulary by using context clues.

1. The new home was built with gutters (wooden drains to collect rainwater from the roof) and downspouts (pipes to drain this rainwater from the roof).

   I think that *gutters and downspouts* are _____

   _____.

2. The tourists were in awe of (amazed by) the incredibly beautiful mountain scenery.

   I think that *in awe of* means _____

   _____.

3. Sofia took the pain medicine the doctor recommended; however, the headaches kept recurring.

   I think that *recurring* means _____

   _____.

4. Parents and children have many obligations (duties) toward each other.

   I think that *obligations* are _____

   _____.

5. The two brothers went to study in a Zen Buddhist temple because they wanted to understand this Buddhist philosophy of inner peace.

   I think that *Zen* is _____

   _____.

6. He felt affirmed (highly valued) when everyone expressed confidence in him.

   I think that *to feel affirmed* means _____

   _____.

7. I can use these old T-shirts as rags to dust the furniture and to protect the rug when we paint.

    I think that *rags* are _____

    _____.

8. The supervisor of the computer department hired Matthew immediately because he demonstrated his knowledge and expertise in advanced computer programming during the interview.

    I think that *expertise* means_____

    _____.

9. Poets are known for their great sensitivity, a strong awareness of feelings and things around them.

    I think that *sensitivity* means _____

    _____.

10. Kwang's job is to escort elderly Asian clients to doctor's appointments because they have no transportation of their own and they need an interpreter for English.

    I think that *to escort* means _____

    _____.

11. The gold-medal winners at the Olympics were very proud of their triumphs (successes).

    I think that *triumphs* are _____

    _____.

12. My parents are exempt from paying federal income taxes because their annual income is too small.

    I think that *exempt* means _____

    _____.

13. The two friends helped each other through every problem in their lives because they had a strong bond (connection) between them.

    I think that a *bond* is_____

    _____.

14. The teacher found many ways to praise the children, like telling them how good their work was and how well they behaved.

    I think that *to praise* means _____

    _____.

15. When we say a person is good at heart but chronically disorganized, we mean that he is a good person and always tries to do his best, but sometimes he has difficulty organizing his life.

    I think that *good at heart but chronically disorganized* means _____

    _____.

16. Barbara owed Joan $50, but Joan let Barbara off the hook by telling her she didn't have to pay it back.

    I think that *letting someone off the hook* means _____

    _____.

17. Americans often use the thumbs-up sign (a gesture consisting of raising up the thumbs of one or both hands) when they want to show congratulations.

    I think the *thumbs-up sign* means_____

    _____.

Vocabulary Quick-Check Review

Check your understanding of the new words and phrases introduced in this chapter by matching the words in Column A with their closest definition in Column B.

Column A	Column B
1. _____ gutters and downspouts	a. tell people how good they are
2. _____ be in awe	b. a strong awareness of feeling
3. _____ recurring	c. duties
4. _____ obligations	d. repeating
5. _____ Zen	e. be amazed
6. _____ feeling affirmed	f. things that collect and drain rainwater
7. _____ rag	g. an Eastern philosophy
8. _____ expertise	h. feeling highly valued
9 _____ .escort	i. old cloth for cleaning
10. _____ triumph	j. a close relationship
11. _____ exempt	k. describes a person who wants to do the right thing
12. _____ bond	l. describes someone who doesn't have to do something that other people must do
13. _____ praise	m. hand gesture showing congratulations
14. _____ sensitivity	n. a lot of knowledge or skill
15 _____ good at heart	o. to take someone somewhere
16. _____ let off the hook	p. when one person decides not to require another person to keep a promise or obligation
17. _____ thumbs up	q. a great success or win

*E*ssay Preview

In the "stick-polishing fantasy" essay, Fulghum introduces us to one of his favorite daydreams. It is also about the subject of living organized or disorganized lives, of doing all the things that a person should do or never do at all! What do you think Fulghum's stick-polishing fantasy is?

*F*ocused Listening

Part 1

Look over the questions in each listening section before you listen to the tape. The questions will give you a general idea about the information contained in the essay. In addition, it will help you focus on the specific information needed to choose the best answer.

The listening exercises are divided into sections. The title of the chapter and the beginning of each listening section are announced by a speaker on the tape. Listen carefully and circle the best answer for each question.

When you've completed listening to Part 1, check your answers on the blackboard together as a whole class. If you wish, you may replay the complete tape—or just specific sections of it.

SECTION I

1. How old was Fulghum when he found out he was supposed to clean gutters and downspouts?
   a. 14.
   b. 45.
   c. 40.

2. Fulghum admires people who
   a. carry heavy things.
   b. put off things.
   c. get things done.

3. Fulghum says these people
   a. never can find what they need.
   b. keep neat files and can always find things.
   c. keep disorganized closets.

4. Fulghum says his daily life is like
   a. a lot of organized people.
   b. a group of monkeys in the zoo.
   c. chasing chickens around a large pen.

SECTION II

5. Fulghum's stick-polishing fantasy begins when
   a. a committee of elders comes to his house.
   b. the Nobel Prize committee comes to his house.
   c. the Academy Award committee welcomes him.

6. The ritual of the polished stick is for people who are
   a. chronically disorganized.
   b. chronically diseased.
   c. chronically late.

7. People who are selected to polish the stick are
   a. good at baseball.
   b. good at heart.
   c. good at speeches.

8. The first thing given to people who are selected to polish the stick is
   a. a week with no obligations.
   b. a week in Hawaii.
   c. a week with a big salary.

9. One performs the ritual of the polished stick in
   a. one's backyard with a loud radio.
   b. a supermarket with a cafeteria.
   c. a very quiet place with Zen.

10. The only job of the person who polishes the stick is
    a. to report daily to the elders.
    b. to polish the stick.
    c. to make phone calls to his or her family.

11. To help the person polish the stick, they give him or her
    a. sandpaper, lemon oil, and rags.
    b. sandpaper and lemons to eat.
    c. sandpaper and a lemon drink.

SECTION III

12. At the end of the week when the ritual of the polished stick is performed,
    a. the elders will steal the stick.
    b. the elders will praise the person's work.
    c. the elders will invite him or her to stay another week.

13. After the person polishes the stick, the newspapers will report
    a. what a good job he or she did.
    b. how long he or she took to polish the stick.
    c. his or her story without a picture.

14. After the stick-polisher returns home, people will be proud and give him or her
    a. a lot of gifts.
    b. a party.
    c. the thumbs-up sign.

SECTION IV

15. After polishing the stick, the stick-polishers can forever
    a. ignore their gutters and downspouts.
    b. ignore their families.
    c. ignore the newspapers.

16. Another benefit from polishing the stick is:
    a. the person wins the lottery.
    b. someone will take care of the stick-polisher's taxes, checkbook, and car.
    c. the person teaches others how to polish the stick.

17. The stick-polisher is also
    a. released from prison.
    b. excused from going to school.
    c. released from the bond of "things to do."

18. Fulghum thinks these benefits
    a. are not enough.
    b. are enough.
    c. are just for a few people.

19. When Fulghum ends the essay saying "Don't I wish," he means
    a. he wishes it were true.
    b. he doesn't want it to be true.
    c. he's very happy it is true.

Part 2

In this listening section, you will listen to the complete essay again, but this time there will be no pauses or narration in between each section.

The sentences below contain information about the essay you just heard. In every sentence, there is some information about the essay which is not true. The information which is not true is <u>underlined</u>. The sentences are listed in the order that the information is heard on the tape. As you listen to the essay again, cross out the incorrect information and write the correct information below it.

1. Fulghum <u>enjoys</u> cleaning his gutters and downspouts every year.

   _____.

2. Fulghum is in awe of people who live <u>disorderly</u> lives.

   _____.

3. Fulghum says that he is also a very <u>orderly</u> person.

   _____.

4. In Fulghum's stick-polishing fantasy, the main goal is to <u>look for</u> a stick.

   _____.

5. In this fantasy, after your job with the stick is completed, the elders will admire your work and <u>take your picture</u>.

   _____.

6. In the stick-polishing fantasy, when you return home all your neighbors and family will <u>ignore</u> you.

   _____.

7. In the stick-polishing fantasy, from this time forward, you will <u>be required</u> to clean your gutters and downspouts.

   _____.

8. Fulghum is <u>happy</u> that his stick-polishing fantasy will never be true.

   _____ .

Listen to the essay again and check your answers with the rest of the class.

$\mathcal{W}$hat Do You Think?

Discuss with your class the answers to the following questions.

1. Why does Fulghum admire people who are very organized? Do you have the same feelings? Why or why not?

2. Describe Fulghum's stick-polishing fantasy. Tell about the details for passing the test. Answer the following questions: Who evaluates the "stick"? Who is chosen to do this? Where does one go to do it?

3. Do you have any favorite daydreams or fantasies that help you pass through difficult or unpleasant times? What are they?

4. Pretend a friend has just locked him/herself out of the house because he/she forgot the house key. Your friend asked you to go through an open window and then open the front door. This is the third time in one year that your friend left the house key in the house and asked you to go through the window to get the key. Your friend is also forgetful about many other things. Do you think you would try to talk to your friend about his/her problems being organized? What advice would you give your friend?

Class Activity

Many Americans have a "wish list," an imaginary list of things they hope to have or do. The beginning of Fulghum's wish list might look like this:

I wish I never had to do another job I didn't like.

Another person's might look like this:

I wish I had a million dollars.
I wish I would meet a handsome man to marry.
I wish I could live in Spain someday.

What would you put on *your* wish list? Write five or more items on the list below. Discuss with your partner why you chose these wishes.

Wish list for _____
              (your name)

I wish _____.

I wish _____.

I wish _____.

I wish _____.

I wish _____.

Reflections: A Cross-Cultural Issue for Discussion or Composition

Cultural Expectations of Excellence

"Excellence" means high quality. Athletes in the Olympic Games strive for "excellence" to win a gold medal and <u>to do</u> their best. "Excellence" is valued highly by many cultures and families within each culture, but expectations of what "excellence" is may vary greatly between cultures.

For example, if a child brought home a report card with three A's (best grade) and one B (second-best grade), some parents might feel very satisfied with his or her school record. Other parents might not be satisfied because the report card contained one B; these parents think "excellence" means all A's.

In your family, what were the expectations for excellence? Was it easy or difficult to satisfy your parents' or relatives' expectations of "excellence"? Is this attitude common throughout your culture, or is it just in your own family?

Prepare an oral report about the expectations of your family, friends, and former teachers regarding "excellence." Include your own expectations of what "excellence" means to you.

Dictation

Listen and fill in the missing words.

At the _____ of the week the _____ will return and they will

_____ your work. They will _____ you for your exper-

tise, your sensitivity, and your _____ insight. "No

_____ was ever _____ quite like *this* !" they will

exclaim. Your _____ will appear on TV and in the papers. You

will be escorted home in _____ triumph. Your _____

and neighbors will give you looks of respect. As you pass in the streets,

people will _____ knowingly and _____ and give you a

_____-____ _____.

Language of Culture: Giving Compliments

Americans give compliments freely. In the essay on the stick-polishing fantasy, the elders evaluating Fulghum's work on polishing the stick compliment him highly by saying "No stick was ever polished quite like this!" Fulghum accepts the compliment and does not argue or disagree with their opinion.

Some newcomers to the United States are surprised and confused by how easily compliments are given in this culture. Americans will often compliment you on how you look (hair or clothes), something you have, something you say, or something you do. Americans expect that when they give you a compliment, you will accept it politely with a "thank you"; they don't expect you to disagree with the compliment even though the custom in many other cultures is to not accept the compliment.

Here's a true example from an ESL class.

Boris: Teacher, did you get back the scores from the English exam we took last week?
Teacher: Yes, Boris. You did extremely well on this difficult exam. There were 37 questions, and you had only one wrong! That's an excellent score!
Boris: One wrong is too much! That's terrible! (Boris argues and does not accept the compliment.)

Here's another example, a conversation between an ESL teacher and a Chinese student named Ling:

Teacher: You look nice today, Ling! (Ling is wearing a new sweater.)
Ling: No, no, teacher. You! You look nice! (Ling does not accept the compliment and then reverses it!)

What do you think of Boris's and Ling's responses to the teacher's compliments? How would you respond?

Here are some general rules about giving and receiving compliments in the United States.

1. Americans expect you to respond in a positive and verbal way to a compliment. If you don't respond to it verbally, you may be considered impolite.

2. If Americans compliment you for something, you do not have to return the compliment immediately. For example, if an American compliments you on the shirt you are wearing, *you* do not have to compliment the American on the shirt *he* is wearing.

3. In some other cultures, if a person compliments something you have, you may be expected to give that person the thing he/she is complimenting. This is *not* true in the United States.

4. Compliments are freely given between parents and children and between employees and employers.

5. Compliments are often used to open or continue a conversation.

How do these customs about compliments compare with those in your culture? In what ways are they different? The same?

The following words and phrases are commonly used to give compliments in American society.

> That's a *great* car!
> That's a *fantastic* car!
> That's a *terrific* car!
> That's an *amazing* car!
> That's an *attractive* car!
> This cake is *wonderful*!
> This cake is *delicious*!
> This cake is *out of this world*!

Here are some common responses to compliments:

> Thanks.
> Thanks for saying that.
> That's very kind of you.
> Thanks. I appreciate that.
> I'm glad you like it (or them).

Let's look at the way compliments can be used to begin or continue conversations:

Judy: Maria, I love the sweater you're wearing! Did you make it yourself?

Maria: Oh, thanks. Well, yes, I did. It took about four months to make.

Judy: I was never really good at crafts. How did you get interested?

Maria: Well, there was an older woman in my neighborhood in Mexico who always invited all the kids in for cookies. We usually helped her with her housekeeping, since she lived alone. Her house was full of hand-made clothes, pillows, blankets, and tablecloths. I asked her to teach me how she made them. We met once a week while I was in high school. I could teach you, if you like!

Judy: Sure! Let's begin!

Please note that when using compliments to open or continue conversations, it is common to put the compliment and/or the response to the compliment into two parts. The first part of Judy's compliment is the thing she is complimenting (the sweater); the second part is a question to extend the compliment into conversation ("Did you make it yourself?"). In the same way, the first part of Maria's response is a form of "thank you"; the second part adds some information ("It took about four months."). Maria herself expresses interest in Judy's compliment, and the two have found a common subject for conversation.

The following are two more examples.

Jeanne: This cake is delicious! May I have the recipe?

Beth: Thanks. I'd be happy to give it to you.

Jeanne: How did you learn to bake?

Beth: Oh, my mother was a great cook. I learned from a master! How about you? Do you enjoy baking?

* * * * *

Burt: You really speak English well!

Elena: Thanks for saying so. I really have a long way to go yet!

Burt: Did you speak English in your native country?

Elena: A little. Do you speak any other languages?

$\mathcal{P}$ractice

Below are the beginnings of two conversations that contain compliments. Fill in the blank sentences to continue the compliments into conversations. Then practice them with a partner.

Paul: The video of your trip to Europe was really great! Did you enjoy using the camera?

Bob: Thanks. Yes, I really liked using it, although it was the first time I had used a video camera. I enjoy photography. How about you?

Paul: I like it, but I don't use my camera a lot. Only a few times a year. It's a 35 mm, not a video camera. Are the video cameras expensive?

Bob: _____

_____

_____

Paul: _____

_____

_____

Bob: _____

_____

_____

Paul: _____

_____

_____

Linda: Beth, your couch is really attractive!

Beth: Oh, I'm glad you like it! I looked around a long time before I bought it.

Linda: The colors and the design are very interesting.

Beth: I read some library books about decorating, and then I went out and started looking for materials to use. Do you enjoy decorating?

Linda: _____
_____
_____

Beth: _____
_____
_____

Linda: _____
_____
_____

Beth: _____
_____
_____

Chapter 8

FATHERS AND SONS

*F*rom generation to generation, parents in all cultures pass their hopes, dreams, and beliefs to their children. The children repeat the same process by passing on to their children their most important beliefs and deepest dreams.

Look at the above illustration and quotation.

- Is there a feeling of movement in the picture?
- If yes, in what direction is the movement?
- Both the quotation and the picture are related to life in the family and also provide clues about the story in this chapter. What do you think the story will be about?
- In what ways are you reminded of your own family life?

Share your thoughts about this with your partner.

About Families

Most people agree that our families influence us in many ways. The family plays a big part in creating an individual's personal and cultural identity. Although family customs and beliefs vary from one culture to another, relationships between family members—such as between parents and children and between sisters and brothers—are sometimes similar.

The family has also been a popular subject in almost all languages. Here are a few English expressions about the influence of the family.

Joe is a chip off the old block. (He's just like one of his parents.)

The acorn doesn't fall far from the tree. (A child becomes like his or her parents.)

Like father, like son. (Whatever the father does, the son will copy.)

About You

What are your feelings about the above expressions? Does your culture have any expressions similar to those listed above? Did your parents or family members use expressions or idioms to describe family life or a particular member of the family?

Try to think of some general idioms about the family in your culture. Write them on the lines below and then exchange papers with a partner.

1. _____

_____

2. _____

_____

3. _____

_____

Your teacher will write on the board all the different idioms from students in your class. In what ways are they different? In what ways are they the same?

Vocabulary Preview Through Context Clues

Before listening to the story about a father and his son, it will be helpful to preview some of the vocabulary you will hear. Previewing unfamiliar vocabulary words and idioms before listening can improve your general comprehension of the story and the events in it.

The sentences below contain new vocabulary words and phrases. Read the sentences carefully and try to figure out the meanings of the new vocabulary by using context clues. Write your ideas on the line below each sentence.

1. The architect built a small-scale model of the building and displayed it in his office because he wanted people to see what the building would look like when the building is finished.

   I think that *small-scale* means _____

   _____.

2. During wartime, many air raids (a time of extreme danger announced by very loud alarms) let people know that danger was near.

   I think that an *air raid* is _____

   _____.

3. Jane and Joe went shopping for things they needed for the new baby, like diapers, baby food, and a crib for the baby to sleep in.

   I think that a *crib* is _____

   _____.

4. When the father is nervous, he paces (walks back and forth over and over) the living room for several hours.

   I think that *to pace* means _____

   _____.

5. The words "to sob" and "to weep" both mean "to cry heavily."

    I think that *to sob* and *to weep* mean _____

    _____.

6. The workers speak sweet, gentle words when they are face to face with their boss. But when the boss is absent, they speak angry words about him and often curse him.

    I think that *to curse* means _____

    _____.

7. People say that Frank is a jerk because he often acts stupidly and foolishly.

    I think that *a jerk* is _____

    _____.

8. After the accident Susan became confused, and when she spoke she was so incoherent that no one could understand what she said.

    I think that *incoherent* means _____

    _____.

9. There was overwhelming evidence that the son and the father were both good people.

    I think that *overwhelming evidence* means _____

    _____.

10. I am going to take my old refrigerator to the store and trade it in (exchange it) for a new model.

    I think that *to trade something in* means _____

    _____.

11. He took the letter in his hand, crumpled it into a ball, and threw it into the trash because he was so angry.

I think that *to crumple something into a ball* means _____

_____.

12. The story of Oedipus, a king in a Greek myth who had a mysterious and violent relationship with his father, is a play that is often studied in college.

I think that *Oedipus* is _____

_____.

13. After the son ran away from home, he never came back to his hometown because he had burned all his bridges behind him and didn't want to see his family again.

I think that *to burn all your bridges behind you* means _____

_____.

14. The Prodigal Son, a story from the New Testament, describes the happiness of a father when his troubled son returns home after many years.

I think that *The Prodigal Son* is _____

_____.

15. The bicycle was upturned on the sidewalk because Diana lost her balance and fell off.

I think that *upturned* means _____

_____.

16. More than twenty people were killed in the train wreck.

I think that a train *wreck* is _____

_____.

$\mathcal{V}$ocabulary Quick-Check Review

Check your understanding of the new words and phrases introduced in this chapter by completing the following matching exercise. Write the letter of the definition from Column B before the word or phrase in Column A that most closely matches the definition.

Column A	Column B
1. ____ small-scale	a. describes something smaller than the original
2. ____ overwhelming evidence	b. not understandable
3. ____ incoherent	c. turned upside down
4. ____ a jerk	d. make into the shape of a ball
5. ____ crumple into a ball	e. to walk back and forth
6. ____ air raid	f. to say mean, dirty words
7. ____ to pace	g. to exchange
8. ____ to curse	h. king in Greek myth
9. ____ to sob, to weep	i. to cry
10. ____ crib	j. story in the New Testament
11. ____ to trade	k. to break all connections with your past life
12. ____ Oedipus	l. baby's bed
13. ____ to burn bridges behind you	m. a warning of danger
14. ____ Prodigal Son	n. clear and definite proof
15. ____ wreck	o. stupid person
16. ____ upturned	p. crash

*E*ssay Preview

The story of this essay involves the relationship of a father and son. The story begins in an American supermarket.

A father is grocery shopping with his three-year-old son. The boy has knocked several bottles of pickles off the shelf, which break when they hit the floor. The son is very upset and won't stop crying. The father is also upset and very frustrated with his son's behavior. In fact, at that moment the father secretly wishes he could run away and not have to take care of his son any more.

As the story continues, this father and son go through many more of life's joyous and painful experiences together. What kind of experiences do you think the story will talk about?

*F*ocused Listening

Part 1

Look over the questions in each listening section before you listen to the tape. The questions will give you a general idea about the information contained in the essay. In addition, it will help you focus on the specific information needed to choose the best answer.

The listening exercises are divided into sections. The title of the chapter and the beginning of each listening section are announced by a speaker on the tape. Listen carefully and circle the best answer for each question.

When you've completed listening to Part 1, check your answers on the blackboard together as a whole class. If you wish, you may replay the complete tape—or just specific sections of it.

SECTION I

1. This story begins in
   a. 1953.
   b. 1963.
   c. 1903.

2. The noise you would hear in the supermarket would sound like
   a. the ocean.
   b. an air raid.
   c. bells.

3. If you saw the mess on the supermarket floor, you would see
   a. a lot of broken pickle jars.
   b. strawberries and blueberries.
   c. a bus wreck.

4. The accident happened to
   a. the father.
   b. the baby.
   c. his three-year-old son.

SECTION II

5. When the father can't control the behavior of his son, he thinks about
   a. calling his home.
   b. getting home fast.
   c. running away from home.

6. The father wants any job that doesn't involve
   a. contact with three-year-olds.
   b. newspapers.
   c. a salary.

7. Temporarily, the father fantasizes
   a. trading in his son for another boy with better behavior.
   b. selling his son to the supermarket.
   c. trading in his son for a new TV.

8. Later, the father sits in his car in the parking lot,
   a. yelling at his son.
   b. trying to remember the way home.
   c. holding his son in his arms until he falls asleep.

9. When the father takes the boy home, he
   a. eats dinner.
   b. puts the boy in his crib.
   c. goes to sleep himself.

10. When the father looks at his sleeping son, he decides
    a. to run away.
    b. to go down to the car again.
    c. not to run away.

SECTION III

11. The man pacing in the living room is holding
    a. his head in his hands.
    b. a letter from his son.
    c. a book to send to his son.

12. The son wrote that
    a. he hates his father and never wants to see him again.
    b. he's coming home soon.
    c. he wants his father to visit him.

13. The son thinks the father is
    a. a failure as a parent.
    b. a failure as a person.
    c. a failure as a teacher.

14. At this time, the father's thoughts about his son are
    a. very happy.
    b. very optimistic.
    c. not very nice.

SECTION IV

15. The father and the son
    a. are both terrible people.
    b. are both good people.
    c. both ran away from home.

16. People say the son is
    a. nothing like his father.
    b. just like his mother.
    c. just like his father.

17. The father shouts "Why did this happen to me?" because
    a. he's so upset.
    b. he wants to share his experiences.
    c. he feels very lucky.

18. It doesn't help the father to explain things because
    a. you have to live through it first.
    b. no one can understand it.
    c. it's clear to everyone.

SECTION V

19. When Fulghum says this story has been lived a thousand times, he means
    a. that stories about the relationship of fathers and sons repeat themselves over and over.
    b. that the story of what happened in the supermarket is not true.
    c. the story of Fulghum writing this book.

20. Fulghum says that even though many stories about fathers and sons have tragic endings like Oedipus, some end like his did. Fulghum's story ended
    a. with the father leaving the son.
    b. with the father and son "burning bridges behind them."
    c. with the son coming back and taking his father in his arms.

21. Fulghum says that the father of the Prodigal Son could tell you this story because
    a. Fulghum is the real father in the story.
    b. Fulghum heard about this story from a friend.
    c. Fulghum wants you to read a book about it.

SECTION VI

22. When we meet the son and father again in 1988, the son is
    a. 28 years old.
    b. 33 years old.
    c. 18 years old.

23. Three mornings a week, you can see the father and his son
    a. skiing.
    b. jogging.
    c. swimming.

24. The son keeps a hand on his father's elbow
    a. to pull him.
    b. to move ahead of him.
    c. to protect him

25. One of their favorite stories is about
    a. giants, wizards and dwarfs.
    b. what happened when the son was born.
    c. what happened in the supermarket twenty-five years ago.

Part 2

In this listening section, you will listen to the complete essay again, but this time there will be no pauses or narration in between each section.

The sentences below contain information about the essay you just heard. In every sentence, there is some information about the essay which is not true. The information which is not true is <u>underlined</u>. The sentences are listed in the order that the information is heard on the tape. As you listen to the essay again, cross out the incorrect information and write the correct information below it.

1. The story about the kid and the pickle jars happens at a <u>gas station</u>.

_____.

2. The father in the story is thinking about <u>returning to the supermarket</u>.

_____.

3. The father is <u>not upset</u> with his son for creating such a mess.

_____.

4. In 1976, according to the story, the son sends his father a <u>very friendly</u> letter.

_____.

5. The father <u>enjoys</u> reading his son's letter.

_____.

6. The son now has his own three-year-old <u>daughter</u>.

_____.

7. In 1988, according to the story, the father and son often <u>swim</u> together.

_____.

8. Fulghum says that the same story of <u>mothers</u> and sons is repeated over and over again all over the world.

_____.

Listen to the tape again and check your answer with the rest of the class.

*W*hat Do You Think?

1. In the story, the father was so upset and embarrassed by his son's behavior he suddenly wanted to run away from his responsibility of being a parent. Do you think this is a common feeling for parents to have? Why or why not? Do you think you would also feel the same if he were your three-year-old son? Why or why not?

2. Fulghum writes that "the father looks at the sleeping child [his son] for a long time. The father does not run away from home." What was the father thinking and feeling then? Why did he change his mind about running away from home?

3. The son wrote a letter to his father telling him he was a terrible father, yet everyone who knows the father and the son agree that they are both good people. Why would the son write a letter like that? Is that surprising to you? If yes, why? Have you ever heard of or known a relationship between a father and son that is similar to the father-son relationship Fulghum describes? If yes, what happened?

4. The son, now in his late twenties, and the father see each other a lot and even jog together three mornings a week. Is this change in their relationship surprising to you? How can such a difficult relationship become so friendly?

*C*lass Activity

Most cultures have important stories about the relationships between fathers and sons and all other family members. Think of a story told or read in your country about the relationship between two or more family members. Tell this story to the class or write the story and later read it to your class.

$\mathcal{R}$eflections: A Key Cross-Cultural Issue for Discussion or Composition

Because the United States is mainly a country of immigrants, many Americans never knew their grandparents and others who stayed behind in the country where their family first lived. Americans often search for their "roots" (or origins) by putting together family histories, often with the help of other relatives and the use of old family photos. Many Americans even visit the family's country to learn more about the history of their family. This helps Americans feel a deeper connection to the whole family and the family traditions, many of which have been forgotten or ignored here in the United States.

Is keeping a record of family history important in your culture? If yes, what are the most common ways people keep these records? Are photographs an important part of these histories?

Prepare an oral presentation or write a composition about how your own family (or families in your culture) keeps records of your family history.

$\mathcal{D}$ictation

Listen and fill in the missing words.

This is 1988.

Same _____ same _____. The son is _____ now,

_____, with his own three-year-old _____, home,

_____, and all the rest. And the father is _____.

Three mornings a week I see them out _____ together around

_____ A.M. As they _____ a busy street, I see the _____

look both ways, with a _____ on his father's _____ to hold

him back from the _____ of oncoming cars, _____ him from

harm. I hear them _____ as they _____ on up the hill into the

_____. And when they sprint toward _____, the son

_____ run ahead, he runs _____ his father at his pace.

They _____ each other a lot. You can _____ it.

They are very careful of each _____ –they have been

_____ a lot _____, but it's all right now.

One of their _____ stories is _____ once upon

a time in a _____ . . . .

*L*anguage of Culture: Ways to Express Surprise or Disbelief

The ways people express their emotions vary greatly from culture to culture. Many new immigrants are often surprised at the openness with which Americans express their emotions. A good example of this can be seen in this chapter's essay about fathers and sons. When the father reads the son's letter, he openly expresses his surprise, hurt, and anger by shouting, "Why did this happen to me?"

If this—or a similar surprising and hurtful situation—happened to a father in your culture, would he be expected to express his painful emotions, or would it be more acceptable for him to keep his emotions hidden?

English has several common expressions that show disbelief or surprise. Americans who want to express surprise at a happy situation may use one of the following expressions:

That's amazing!   It's incredible!
You're kidding!   You're pulling my leg!
I don't believe it!   I can't believe it!
That's great!   Wow!

If Americans hear bad or unfortunate news, it is common to respond with one of the following expressions.

It can't be!   No!
I had no idea!   What a shame!
Oh, my God!   That's too bad!

Have you heard any other expressions of surprise or disbelief in English? If so, what are they?

Read the following short dialogues and decide whether the expressions used in answer to the first speaker are spoken in response to happy or bad news.

Mary: Jennifer, I want to tell you some good news. Joe and I have decided to get married.
Jennifer: (Surprised) That's great!

Michael: I just got the scores back from our math test.
Lenny: How did you do?
Michael: I got the best grade in the class.
Lenny: That's amazing!

Julia: Margie, you seem upset. Is anything wrong?
Margie: My mother had a heart attack last week, and she is having a slow recovery.
Julia: Oh, I had no idea!

Gary: Did you hear why our history teacher is absent?
Mitch: No.
Gary: His son disappeared in the mountains on a camping trip last weekend. They haven't been able to find him.
Mitch: Oh, my God!

Practice 1

Respond to the following statements with an expression of surprise for happy or bad news. Use some of the expressions mentioned in the previous section. First write your answer. Then read the statements to your partner and ask him or her to respond orally to them.

Examples:

I just found out I failed the entrance exams to go to college.
<u>What a shame!</u>

My sister just gave birth to a baby girl!
<u>Wow!</u>

1. I just won $500 in a writing contest!.

   _____.

2. I lost my job two weeks ago and don't have enough money to pay the rent.

   _____.

3. I just heard that my son is coming to visit me from out of town.

   _____.

4. After I escaped from my country, I never heard from my family again.

   _____.

5. My gold watch was stolen from the laboratory today.

   _____.

𝒫ractice 2

Below are some responses of surprise. Before each response, fill in the rule with an appropriate statement.

Examples:

<u>My son will be hospitalized for six months because of kidney problems.</u>
I had no idea!

<u>I got an '"A"in every course.</u>
You're kidding!

1. _____.

   "It can't be!"

2. _____.

   "You're pulling my leg!"

3. _____.

   "What a shame!"

4. _____.

   "It's incredible!"

5. _____.

   "I had no idea!"

"I had the feeling I was walking the earth in a totally new way. The earth had become more intimate, more alive . . ."
—Henry Miller, *The Colossus of Marousi*

Chapter 9

DONNIE AND THE SENSES

𝒜s the seasons change, we become aware of the passing of time and how fast the years disappear. Too often we are impatient for the seasons to pass, and we may miss the many meanings and sensations that each season has to offer us.

Look at the illustration on this page. Try to smell the leaves and feel the autumn air.

- Can you identify all the things that you see in the picture?
- In what ways does this picture suggest a special relationship between nature and the senses?
- What hidden messages are revealed in the different shapes of the leaves?
- In what ways can our senses awaken us to new experiences?

How are these ideas related to the quotation above the picture and the picture itself?

About the Senses

There are many ways to think about and use our senses. Most of the information we get about the world comes through our senses. Each of us feels things differently and learns things differently according to our unique internal sensing equipment. Some people learn best by seeing things, others learn best from hearing things, and still others learn best by doing things.

Everyone has his or her own way to receive messages through his or her senses. People are often surprised to find out that Beethoven wrote some of his last, most difficult music when he was deaf. Many people feel it was tragic that he couldn't hear his Ninth Symphony. Do you think hearing takes place only with the ears? Do you think he could have "heard" the music in his head and known how it sounded even though he was deaf?

In the musical *The Fantasticks*, the actors invite the audience to think back to an earlier time in their lives and imagine a beautiful day they might have had in a lovely forest or woods. They suggest you imagine it:

> Not with your eyes, for they are wise;
> But see it with your ears:
> The cool green breathing of the leaves.
> And hear it with the inside of your hands.

About You

What are your thoughts about the ways we can use our senses? Do you think it is possible to "hear" with your hands or "see" with your ears? What are your ideas about Beethoven writing music while he was deaf? Do you think it is possible to "see" a forest with your ears?

Describe experiences you have had which demonstrate unusual ways people use their senses. Which sense or senses do you think you use the most for learning? Describe your experiences and ideas about our senses to another student.

$\mathcal{V}$ocabulary Quick-Check Review

Check your understanding of the new words and phrases introduced in this chapter by completing the following matching exercise. Write the letter of the definition from Column B that matches the word or phrase in Column A.

Column A	**Column B**
1. _____ scrawled	a. describing someone who can't hear
2. _____ ravine	b. to give up
3. _____ twilight	c. written poorly and hard to understand
4. _____ deaf	d. the time just before dark
5. _____ to sign	e. describing someone who has difficulty saying what he or she wants to say
6. _____ a compost heap	f. to move your head up and down
7. _____ to hold on	g. a small canyon
8. _____ cynical	h. pessimistic
9. _____ inarticulate	i. to continue what you are doing in difficult circumstances
10. _____ takes pride in	j. a pile of leftover grass and leaves used for fertilizer
11. _____ to nod	k. to communicate in a language of hand signals
12. _____ to let go	l. feels proud about

*E*ssay Preview

This chapter's essay, "Donnie and the Leaves," begins in autumn. The leaves on the trees are changing colors and falling to the ground. Fulghum likes to see the leaves spread naturally all across his backyard. (In a part of the essay not included on the tape, Fulghum describes a conflict about this subject between him and his wife. Fulghum's wife likes neat piles of raked leaves, which Fulghum does not. This year Fulghum and his wife have decided to compromise by doing a scientific experiment. They have agreed to rake half the yard and leave the other half unraked.) Fulghum changes his mind about raking only half of the yard when Donnie, a deaf boy in the neighborhood, comes to the front door. Donnie has been going around the neighborhood looking for customers who would like to have their leaves raked. Fulghum learns a lot about the relationship between nature and our senses when he hires Donnie. Why do you think Fulghum decided to let Donnie rake his leaves?

*F*ocused Listening

Part 1

Look over the questions in each listening section before you listen to the tape. The questions will give you a general idea about the information contained in the essay. In addition, it will help you focus on the specific information needed to choose the best answer.

The listening exercises are divided into sections. The titles of the chapter and the beginning of each listening section are announced by a speaker on the tape. Listen carefully and circle the best answer for each question.

When you've completed listening to Part 1, check your answers on the blackboard together as a whole class. If you wish, you may replay the complete tape—or just specific sections of it.

SECTION I

1. Fulghum ran quickly to open the door because
   a. he thought it might be an emergency.
   b. he wanted to say hello to Donnie.
   c. he was in a hurry to get to work.

2. When he got to the door, he saw
   a. a policeman.
   b. a soldier.
   c. a small boy.

3. Donnie handed Fulghum
   a. a rake.
   b. a note.
   c. a pile of leaves.

4. Donnie wrote notes to Fulghum because
   a. he writes very well.
   b. it's a good business technique.
   c. he cannot hear.

SECTION II

5. Donnie reminded Fulghum of
   a. a pilot not using any instruments.
   b. a pilot who couldn't use instruments.
   c. a pilot depending on instruments, not vision.

6. Donnie thinks Fulghum might let him rake his leaves because
   a. he has seen many leaves in Fulghum's backyard.
   b. he heard Fulghum wants to have someone rake his leaves.
   c. he asked Fulghum before.

7. Donnie holds out his pencil and paper for
   a. Fulghum's signature.
   b. Fulghum's address.
   c. Fulghum's answer.

8. Donnie's note said he charges
   a. $1.50 a yard.
   b. $1.00 a yard.
   c. $1.75 a yard.

SECTION III

9. While Donnie waits for Fulghum's answer, Fulghum wonders what he would do
   a. if Donnie couldn't see.
   b. if Donnie weren't deaf.
   c. if Donnie never came to the door.

10. Finally, Fulghum writes that
     a. Donnie should go home.
     b. he doesn't want his leaves raked.
     c. he wants his leaves raked.

11. When Fulghum asks Donnie if he rakes the leaves when they are wet, Donnie writes,
     a. yes.
     b. no.
     c. sometimes.

12. How much money does Fulghum agree to pay Donnie?
     a. $3.50.
     b. $3.25.
     c. $3.00.

SECTION IV

13. Donnie begins raking the leaves
     a. the next day.
     b. right away.
     c. after one hour.

14. Fulghum watches Donnie and wonders if
     a. Donnie thinks about sound.
     b. there are any sounds in Donnie's mind.
     c. Donnie sings in his mind.

15. Fulghum puts his fingers in his ears to try
     a. to hear the sea.
     b. to experience being deaf.
     c. to measure sound.

16. Fulghum thinks Donnie is a good worker because he
     a. charges a lot of money.
     b. borrowed Fulghum's rake.
     c. rakes all the leaves.

SECTION V

17. Donnie signed to Fulghum that
     a. it was dark, but he wanted to keep working.
     b. it was dark, and he was tired.
     c. it was dark, and he had to go home.

18. Fulghum doubted Donnie would come back to finish the job because
    a. he refused to pay him.
    b. he didn't pay him yet.
    c. he had already paid him.

19. Donnie came back the next morning
    a. and asked for money.
    b. and finished his job.
    c. and handed Fulghum another note.

20. Fulghum saw Donnie pick up some yellow leaves and
    a. put them in his sweatshirt.
    b. throw them away.
    c. put them under the tree.

SECTION VI

21. Donnie came to Fulghum's door and signed that
    a. he needed another rake.
    b. he wanted more money.
    c. the work was done.

22. Fulghum said that tomorrow he would push the pile of leaves
    a. all over his yard again.
    b. into the compost heap.
    c. to Donnie's house.

23. When Fulghum said "The leaves let go, the seeds let go, and I must let go sometimes, too," he meant
    a. he sometimes has to let go of an opinion or an idea.
    b. the trees sometimes let go of all their leaves.
    c. he will never change his mind.

24. When Fulghum said, "Hold on, Donnie, hold on," he was telling Donnie
    a. don't work so hard.
    b. don't ever give up.
    c. don't rake leaves any more.

Part 2

In this listening section, you will listen to the complete essay again, but this time there will be no pauses or narration in between each section.

The sentences below contain information about the essay you just heard. In every sentence, there is some information about the essay which is not true. The information which is not true is <u>underlined</u>. The sentences are listed in the order that the information is heard on the tape. As you listen to the essay again, cross out the incorrect information and write the correct information below it.

1. When Donnie comes to Fulghum's door, he hands him a <u>broom</u>.

   _____.

2. Fulghum is surprised Donnie wants to rake the leaves because <u>there are not many leaves in his yard</u>.

   _____.

3. Donnie agrees to rake the leaves in Fulghum's yard for <u>$2.50</u>.

   _____.

4. While Fulghum watches Donnie rake the leaves, he wonders what it is like to be <u>blind</u>.

   _____.

5. Fulghum is <u>sure</u> that Donnie will return the next day to finish raking the leaves.

   _____.

6. Donnie <u>does not return</u> to finish raking the leaves the next day.

   _____.

7. Fulghum thinks that Donnie <u>hates</u> raking and playing with the leaves.

   _____.

8. After Donnie left, Fulghum raked the pile of leaves into the <u>garage</u>.

   _____.

Listen to the essay again and check your answer with the rest of the class.

*W*hat Do You Think?

Discuss with your class the answers to the following questions.

1. Why do you think Fulghum let Donnie rake his leaves? If Donnie came to your front door, would you do the same thing as Fulghum did? Why or why not?

2. What are your impressions about Donnie? Does he remind you of anyone you ever knew? If so, describe that person and explain why Donnie reminds you of him/her.

3. Go back and look at the illustration at the beginning of this chapter. Do you see more in the picture than you saw the first time you looked at it? Look at the shapes of all the leaves. In what ways are these leaves related to Donnie? How do theses leaves represent our senses?

*C*lass Activity

Educators say that each individual has a specific learning style. Studies show that these learning styles are based on our senses and that most individuals use only one or two of these senses most of the time. Here are three examples of learning styles.

1. Visual – A visual learner learns best by seeing or looking at things. These people learn best by using charts and pictures.

2. Auditory – An auditory learner likes to talk and listen. These people learn best by listening to stories, TV, and radio.

3. Kinesthetic-Tactile – A kinesthetic-tactile learner likes to touch and feel things. These people learn best by taking things apart and putting them together. They also like a lot of movement and activity and they learn by doing things.

Which of these learning styles best describes the way you learn? Describe your learning style to your partner or the class and give an example of something you learned recently using this method.

$\mathcal{R}$eflections: A Cross-Cultural Issue for Discussion or Composition

During the past twenty-five years, the U.S. Congress has passed many laws requiring equal opportunity for all physically disabled persons who are seeking a job, education, and housing. Increased attention to the special needs of people with disabilities has made Americans more aware of the problems of the handicapped. The government programs that have been developed in the past three decades encourage disabled Americans to become an active part of society. This demonstrates a big change from the attitudes of thirty years ago, when disabled Americans were expected to live lonely, separate lives apart from society.

What is the attitude of your culture about disabled people? Do they live separately from the rest of society or are they part of the general society? What is your opinion about how society should treat people who are disabled? What are your personal ideas about this subject?

Prepare an oral presentation on this subject for your class or write a composition explaining your answers to the above questions.

$\mathcal{D}$ictation

Listen and fill in the missing words.

_____ that he must go because it is dark and he must go

_____ to eat, he leaves the work _____. Having _____

in advance, I _____ if he will return. At age _____, I am

cynical. Too cynical. Come _____, he has _____ to his task

first _____ the previously raked yard for latecomers. He takes

_____ in his work. The yard is _____ _____. I note his

_____ up several of the brightest _____ _____ and

putting them into the _____ of his sweat shirt.

$\mathcal{L}$anguage of Culture: Nonverbal Communication

Every culture has body movements and gestures that communicate messages without words. This form of communication is called "nonverbal communication"—or communication without words.

In the story about Donnie, notice that both Fulghum and Donnie use a lot of nonverbal communication in their agreement about raking the leaves. First, Donnie holds out a paper for Fulghum to read. Then, Donnie offers Fulghum a pencil for an answer. After Fulghum writes, "Yes, I would like to have my leaves raked," Fulghum gets "a grave nod" from Donnie (the boy moves his head up and down, meaning "okay"). After the two agree on three dollars ($3.00) for the job, Donnie "grins" (smiles) at Fulghum. With few words spoken or written, Donnie and Fulghum have come to an agreement using mainly nonverbal communication.

When you first arrive in a new culture, it is often more difficult to understand nonverbal communication than it is to understand the spoken language. The following is a true story illustrating how easy it is for a new immigrant to misunderstand nonverbal communication.

Minh, a refugee from Vietnam, was in a training class to learn auto repair. One day he asked his instructor a question. As the teacher began to answer Minh's question, the teacher took a piece of paper, crumbled it up in his hand, and threw it into the trash basket. Although this action had no meaning to the teacher, to Minh it had a clear meaning. In Vietnam, if someone crumbles up a piece of paper in front of you and then throws it out, it means that person is very angry with you. Minh couldn't understand why the teacher was angry with him. So he spoke with an American student in the class about what had happened. Much to Minh's surprise, the American told him that the teacher's action had nothing to do with Minh and that the teacher wasn't angry at all. Minh asked the teacher directly. The instructor apologized to Minh and said his action had no meaning. He was just throwing out a piece of paper.

It is possible that crumbling up a piece of paper and throwing it out *could* be a sign of anger in U.S. culture, but if this happened, the person would probably show *anger* through a facial expression. In Vietnam, the *action* is most important; crumbling up a piece of paper, throwing it out, and *smiling* would probably still mean that the person was angry.

This example shows how a simple gesture can lead to misunderstanding. The list below indicates a few general hints to help you understand nonverbal communication in U.S. culture.

1.   American culture is a very verbal culture. In most situations, Americans speak directly to each other and use direct language to communicate. Unlike many other cultures, Americans ask questions in school and on the job if they don't understand something. It is often difficult for newcomers to the United States to understand this. If you keep quiet about something that you don't understand, Americans will think you do understand it.

2.   During a conversation, Americans are generally uncomfortable with silence. They will try to break the silence with some kind of talk.

3.   Americans may not understand the silence of newcomers. It is best to respond to Americans with some sort of verbal statement. Remember that the forms of nonverbal communication in the United States are different from those in your culture.

Practice

Answer the following True-False questions about nonverbal communication. Write "True" if the statement is true. If the statement is false, write "False" and, on the line below, explain why the statement is false.

1.   Americans feel uncomfortable with silence during a conversation.

   _____

   _____.

2.   Nonverbal communication is easy to understand in all cultures.

   _____

   _____.

3.   If you don't know how to do something on your job in the United States, it's best not to tell anyone.

   _____

   _____.

4. In the United States, if someone asks you a question about something you don't know, just smile and don't answer.

   _____

   _____.

5. Minh's auto repair teacher was angry at Minh.

   _____

   _____.

6. Minh was wrong to ask the teacher if he was angry at him.

   _____

   _____.

7. Although Fulghum and Donnie used nonverbal communication, they understood each other well.

   _____

   _____.

There's no use trying," she said. "One can't believe impossible things."

"You haven't had much practice," said the Queen (to Alice). "When I was your age, I always did it for half-an-hour a day. — sometimes I've believed as many as six impossible things before breakfast."
— Lewis Carroll, *Alice in Wonderland*

Chapter 10

LARRY WALTERS AND HIS FLYING DREAM MACHINE

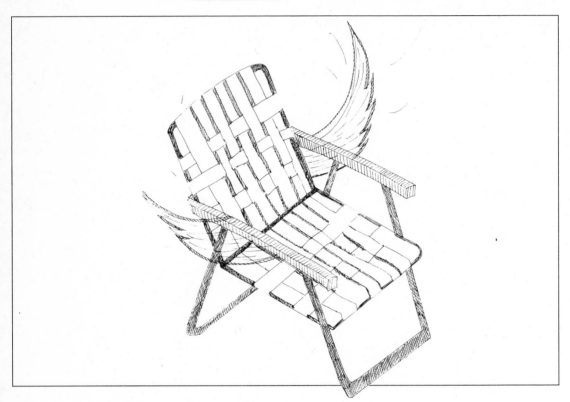

*A*re you a person who believes "impossible things" like the Queen in *Alice in Wonderland*? There may be as many "impossible things" to believe as there are people in the world! One very popular "impossible thing" throughout human history has been the desire of individuals to fly through the air like a bird. We all know that flying an airplane is possible, but how about other ways for humans to fly?

Discuss the following questions with your partner.

• Have you (or anyone you have known) wished you could fly like a bird? If yes, why do you think this wish is important?

- Have you ever heard of people who really tried to fly? If yes, how did they try to do it?
- The illustration shows clues about the story in this chapter. What do you think the story is about?
- In what ways do you think the illustration and the quotation above the picture are related?

About Personal Dreams

The personal dreams of just one person can influence the actions and thoughts of many people. Most every country has famous individuals whose unforgettable words or actions have changed their country or the world in some way.

In the United States, there have been many special people whose words and actions made American society a better place. These people all had a dream of making a better America, even though they faced many difficulties, their words and actions made their dream a reality. Susan B. Anthony, for example, had a dream of an America where women could vote. (Before 1920, only men could vote in the U.S.) In addition to successfully working with other Americans to end slavery, this brave woman devoted the rest of her life to convincing the U.S. government to allow women to vote. Largely because of her words and actions, the nineteenth amendment to the U.S. Constitution, which gave voting rights to all American women twenty-one years and older, was made law in 1920.

Helen Keller was another remarkable person who had a dream and made it come true. Even though she was deaf and blind as a child, she had a dream to be able to read, write, and communicate with other people. So she learned to read and write—and she even learned sign language to communicate with deaf people. Her success in dealing with her many disabilities, in addition to her published writings, inspired* many Americans, making them aware of the needs and successes of all disabled people.

One of the most famous Americans of the twentieth century, Martin Luther King, also had a dream. He was a black American minister who dreamed of a world without racism** and war. His nonviolent actions

*Inspired—to be encouraged.
**Racism—hate toward someone because of his or her skin color.

and his powerful words helped end racial segregation and helped protect the voting rights of black Americans in some southern states of the United States during the 1950s and 1960s. In one of his most famous speeches, he spoke about his dearest dreams:

> I say to you today, my friends, that in spite of the difficulties and frustrations of the moment I still have a dream. It is a dream deeply rooted in the American dream. I have a dream that one day this nation will rise up and live out the true meaning of its creed: "We hold these truths to be self-evident; that all men are created equal. " I have a dream that my four little children will one day live in a nation where they will not be judged by the color of their skin but by the content of their character. I have a dream today.

> Speech at the Washington Monument,
> Washington, D.C., August 28, 1963

About You

Have you ever heard of Susan B. Anthony, Helen Keller, or Martin Luther King, Jr.? Were you surprised about any information you read about them? How do you feel about the words and message of Martin Luther King? Are his words important for you personally?

Does reading this passage of Dr. King's speech remind you of any person in your country whose dreams have changed the lives of other people? Think about it for a few moments and then share your thoughts with a classmate.

Ask your partner to share some special dreams about his or her country or personal life.

Vocabulary Preview Through Context Clues

Before listening to the story about Larry Walters on tape, it will be helpful to preview some of the vocabulary you will hear in the story. Previewing unfamiliar vocabulary words and idioms before listening to each chapter's essay can improve your general comprehension of the story and the events in it.

The sentences below contain the new vocabulary words and phrases in this chapter's essay. Read the sentences carefully and try to figure out the meanings of the words and phrases by using context clues.

1. Kids love to pop balloons after a birthday party because they like to hear the noise made by the balloons when they explode and fall to the ground.

   I think *to pop* means _____

   _____.

2. Christopher Columbus surprised the cynics (pessimists) who didn't believe he could sail around the world.

   I think *a cynic* is _____

   _____.

3. Birds have many beautiful movements, such as flapping their wings up and down when they fly.

   I think *flapping* means _____

   _____.

4. Many dangerous and exciting sports are becoming popular, like hang gliding (wearing cloth wings and jumping off a hill) and sky diving (jumping out of a plane and falling some distance before opening the parachute).

   I think *hang gliding* is _____

   _____.

5. We took all the surplus food left over from the wedding to the church so the extra food could be distributed to hungry people.

   I think *surplus* means _____

   _____.

6. The doctor gave a few suggestions to Joan to help her get more energy, such as taking vitamin and mineral supplements.

   I think *vitamin and mineral supplements* are _____

   _____.

7. The people didn't understand his behavior and thought he was a maniac, a person with behavior that he can't control.

I think a *maniac* is _____

_____.

8. We knew that Lucille had just heard the good news about her daughter because she was grinning from ear to ear, and her smile made us very happy.

I think *grinning from ear to ear* means _____

_____.

9. Jim is usually a very talkative person; however, last night he was taciturn and kept his thoughts to himself.

I think *taciturn* means _____

_____.

10. Although Juanita didn't pass the course, her father told her that what counts (what's important) is that she tried to do her best.

I think *"what counts"* means _____

_____.

11. Lawn chairs, chairs with colored plastic strips of webbing nailed onto a metal frame, are very popular for backyard use.

I think *plastic strips of webbing* are _____

_____.

Vocabulary Quick-Check Review

Check your understanding of the new vocabulary words and phrases introduced in this chapter by completing the following matching exercises. Write the letter of the definition in Column B that matches the word or phrase in Column A.

Column A	Column B
1. _____ hang gliding	a. extra
2. _____ webbing	b. not speaking; quiet
3. _____ taciturn	c. plastic strips for a chair
4. _____ maniac	d. pills for energy and health
5. _____ a cynic	e. moving arms or wings up and down
6. _____ to flap	f. a pessimistic person
7. _____ surplus	g. a dangerous sport
8. _____ "what counts"	h. a person with strange and uncontrolled behavior
9. _____ a grin from ear to ear	i. to explode or make a hole
10._____ vitamin and mineral supplements	j. the thing that's most important
11. _____ to pop	k. a big smile

Essay Preview

For many years, Larry Walters sat on a lawn chair in his backyard, looking up at the sky and dreaming about flying. After several years of thinking about this dream, he finally decided to do it. The way he decided to do it and what happened when he did it are the subjects of this essay. How do you think Larry made his dream come true?

$\mathcal{F}$ocused Listening

Part 1

Look over the questions in each listening section before you listen to the tape. The questions will give you a general idea about the information contained in the essay. In addition, it will help you focus on the specific information needed to choose the best answer.

The listening exercises are divided into sections. The title of the chapter and the beginning of each listening section are announced by a speaker on the tape. Listen carefully and circle the best answer for each question.

When you've completed listening to Part 1, check your answers on the blackboard together as a whole class. If you wish, you may replay the complete tape—or just specific sections of it.

SECTION I

1. Larry Walters is
   a. a truck driver.
   b. a race car driver.
   c. a bus driver.

2. Larry's wish is
   a. to quit work.
   b. to make a lot of money.
   c. to fly.

3. Larry Walters wanted to be a pilot, but
   a. he didn't have the time, money, or opportunity.
   b. his parents discouraged him.
   c. he became afraid.

4. He didn't go hang gliding because it was
   a. too dangerous.
   b. too expensive.
   c. too difficult.

5. According to the tape, old aluminum lawn chairs usually have
   a. rivets and pillows.
   b. webbing and wood frames.
   c. webbing and rivets.

SECTION II

6. When Larry Walters flew over Los Angeles in his lawn chair,
    a. the newspapers and TV did not report his story.
    b. the newspapers and TV reported the story.
    c. only the newspapers reported his story.

7. His lawn chair was flying because
    a. he had connected it to a helicopter.
    b. he had connected it to an airplane.
    c. he had connected it to weather balloons.

8. Larry took these things on the trip with him:
    a. a parachute and a C.B. radio.
    b. a C.B. radio and a tunafish sandwich.
    c. a B.B. gun and 12 cans of beer.

9. His lawn chair flew near
    a. Disneyland.
    b. the Los Angeles Airport.
    c. the Pacific Ocean.

SECTION III

10. He told reporters that the reason he did it was that
    a. he enjoys flying in balloons.
    b. he can hear his radio better in the air.
    c. you can't just sit there forever in the backyard.

11. When Larry spoke to reporters,
    a. he had a long speech prepared.
    b. he answered questions with just a few words.
    c. he asked them not to take pictures.

12. When reporters asked him if he would do it again, he said
    a. "Yes."
    b "Nope."
    c. "Maybe."

SECTION IV

13. Fulghum says that "the human race sits in its chair" and that
    a. some people think we cannot change anything, but other
       people continue to dream about new ways to do things.
    b. all people feel changing the human race is hopeless.
    c. all people have great hope for the future.

14. Fulghum thinks that Larry Walters showed that
    a. anything is possible.
    b. nothing unusual is possible.
    c. wishes never come true.

15. Fulghum believes that
    a. imagination is not an important part of being human.
    b. the spirit doesn't count.
    c. the spirit counts a lot.

SECTION V

16. Fulghum says there will always be cynics who say
    a. human beings don't want to fly.
    b. human beings can't fly.
    c. human beings have the ability to fly.

17. Fulghum says that even though human beings really can't fly,
    a. there will never be human beings who want to fly.
    b. there will always be some maniac who will keep trying to fly.
    c. all human beings will fly someday.

Part 2

In this listening section, you will listen to the complete essay again, but this time there will be no pauses or narration in between each section.

The sentences below contain information about the essay you just heard. In every sentence, there is some information about the essay which is not true. The information which is not true is <u>underlined</u>. The sentences are listed in the order that the information is heard on the tape. As you listen to the essay again, cross out the incorrect information and write the correct information below it.

1. In this story, Larry Walters is a very <u>old</u> man.

   _____.

2. Larry Walters spent a lot of his time sitting in his <u>car</u>, thinking about being able to fly.

   _____.

3. Larry Walters wanted to be a <u>doctor</u>, but he did not have the money or the opportunity to be one.

_____.

4. Larry Walters flew up in the air over the skies of <u>New York</u>.

_____.

5. Larry Walters was a man who really <u>liked to talk</u> a lot.

_____.

6. Fulghum thinks there are <u>not</u> many people like Larry Walters who try to make their dreams come true.

_____.

7. Fulghum thinks that people's spirits are <u>not important</u> to make dreams come true.

_____.

8. Fulghum thinks that <u>money</u> is very important for a person's dreams.

_____.

Listen to the essay again and check your answers with the rest of the class.

*W*hat Do You Think?

Discuss with your class the answers to the following questions:

1. Did anything about Larry Walters and his flying lawn chair surprise you? What surprised you? Why do you think it surprised you?

2. Do you think the day that Larry Walters flew in his chair was an important day in his life? Why or why not?

3. When the reporters asked him if he had enjoyed the trip, he said "yes." But when they asked him if he wanted to do it again, he said "no." Why do you think he answered that way?

Class Activity

If Larry Walters were a good friend of yours and he wrote to ask your advice about whether he should try to fly in his lawn chair, what advice would you give him? Would you tell him to keep trying to find a way to do it, or would you tell him to give up the idea?

Think carefully about your answer to this question. Write down a few of your ideas on paper. Then, with a partner or a group, write a letter to Larry Walters telling him your advice about this situation. Whether you encourage him or discourage him, be very clear about explaining your opinion. When you've completed the letter, share it with other students in the class.

Use this model to begin the letter.

(Date) _____

Dear Larry,

It was good to hear from you the other day. I'm very happy to give you advice about your idea of flying in your lawn chair.

First, _____

_____.

Second, _____

_____.

Third, _____

_____

_____.

Write back soon.

Your friend(s),

_____

$\mathcal{R}$eflections: A Cross-Cultural Issue for Discussion or Composition

In general, Americans celebrate individuality. This can be seen throughout U.S. culture in history, sports, and education. American heroes and heroines are frequently people who do things alone like Larry Walters, doing things that haven't been done before (such as attaching balloons to a lawn chair and flying across the highway).

Although many areas of U.S. culture focus on individual rather than group goals (or dreams), this is not the case in many other cultures. In those cultures, the needs and interests of the group are more important. Members of those societies are taught from an early age to put aside their own desires for the benefit of the group (for example, family and government) and not to do anything to look different from anyone else.

In your own culture, are people encouraged to be different? What are your personal ideas about this? Do you agree or disagree with the attitudes expressed about individuality in your culture? What are your ideas about the expression of individuality in much of U.S. culture?

Prepare an oral presentation about your ideas concerning individuality to share with the class, or write a composition on the same subject.

$\mathcal{D}$ictation

Listen and fill in the missing words.

It's the _____ here that counts. The time may be long, the vehicle

may be _____ or unexpected. But if the _____ is held close to

the heart, and _____ is applied to what there is close at hand,

everything is still _____.

But wait! Some _____ from the edge of the crowd insists that

human beings still _____ _____ fly. Not like birds, anyway.

_____. But somewhere in some little garage, some _____ with

a gleam in his eye is scarfing vitamin and _____ supplements, and

practicing _____ his arms faster and faster, and faster, and who

knows?

*L*anguage of Culture: Ways to Ask Open-Ended Questions

One problem common to new language learners is how to keep a conversation moving. They often feel embarrassed and lack confidence about how to ask questions when a conversation stops or pauses.

It is helpful to recognize that in English and many other languages, two main types of questions are used. The first is a yes or no question, which means that the person answering the question will answer "yes" or "no." The second kind of question is an open-ended question. The person answering this kind of question can answer in a very "open" or broad way. Look at these two examples from this essay.

Example A:

The reporters asked Larry Walters: "Why did you do it?"
Walters answered: "You just can't sit there."

Example B:

The reporters asked Larry Walters: "Would you do it again?"
Larry Walters: "Nope." (slang for "no")

Which question—Example A or Example B—offers the most opportunity for broad answers? (Circle your choice.) If you are trying to keep a conversation moving, which question do you think is best? Discuss your answer with your class.

A technique to create open-ended questions is to practice asking questions that begin with "what," "how," "why," "when," or "who. Look at these examples.

What do you think of my new car?
What do you think of our new boss?
What do you think of the new schedule?

How do you feel about working overtime?
How do you feel about American food?
How do you feel about American TV?

I like to eat Italian food. How about you?
I think our homework was very difficult. What do you think?

$\mathcal{P}$ractice

Change these yes-no questions to open-ended ones.

Examples:

Yes-no

Do you like American music?

Did they like the trip?

Open-ended

How do you feel about American music?

How was their trip?

1. Do you like to play baseball?

   _____?

2. Does my brother like to cook?

   _____?

3. Do you like to practice English?

   _____?

4. Do I like to eat?

   _____?

5. Do the children like our pets?

   _____?

Sit with your partner. Each of you should write five more yes-no questions. Exchange these questions and have each partner change the yes-no questions to open-ended ones. Then answer each other's questions on paper.

Tapescript

Chapter 1

It Was on Fire When I Lay Down on It

A tabloid newspaper carried the story, stating simply that a small-town emergency squad was summoned to a house where smoke was pouring from an upstairs window. The crew broke in and found a man in a smoldering bed. After rescuing him and dousing the mattress, the obvious question was asked: "How did this happen?"

"I don't know. It was on fire when I lay down on it."

It was on fire when I lay down on it.

A lot of us could settle for that on our tombstone. A life-story in a sentence. Out of the frying pan and into the hot water. I was looking for trouble and I got into it as soon as I found it. The devil made me do it the first time, and after that I did it on my own.

Or to point at this truth at a less intense level, I report a conversation with a colleague who was complaining that he had the same damn stuff in his lunch sack day after day after day.

"So who makes your lunch?" I asked.

"I do," says he.

Oh and one more thing.

About the man in the burning bed in the story. As with most of what we see other people do, we really don't know why they do it. If our own actions are mysteries, how much so others'? Why did he lie down on the burning bed? Was he drunk? Ill? Suicidal? Blind? Cold? Dumb? Did he just have a weird sense of humor? Or what? I don't know. It's hard to judge without a lot more information. Oh sure, we go ahead and judge anyhow. But maybe if judgment were suspended a bit more often, we would like us more.

God, it is written, warned his first children, Adam and Eve. He made it clear. Don't eat that piece of fruit—it will lead to trouble. You know the rest of that story . . .

And part of the rest of that story is here in this tape.

Chapter 2
The Mermaid

Giants, Wizards, and Dwarfs was the game to play.

Being left in charge of about eighty children seven to ten years old, while their parents were off doing parenty things, I mustered my troops in the church social hall and explained the game. It's a large-scale version of Rock, Paper, and Scissors, and involves decision making. But the real purpose of the game is to make a lot of noise and run around chasing people until nobody knows which side you are on or who won.

I yelled out: "You have to decide *now* which you are—a GIANT, a WIZARD, or a DWARF!"

And while the groups huddled in consultation, a tug came at my pants leg. A small child stood there looking up, and asked in a small, concerned voice, "Where do the Mermaids stand?"

Where do the Mermaids stand?

A long pause. A *very* long pause. "Where do the Mermaids stand?" says I.

"Yes. You see, I am a Mermaid."

"There are no such things as Mermaids."

"Oh, yes, I am one!"

She did not relate to being a Giant, a Wizard, or a Dwarf. She knew her category. Mermaid. And was not about to leave the game and go over and stand against the wall where a loser would stand. She intended to participate, wherever Mermaids fit into the scheme of things. Without giving up dignity or identity. She took it for granted that there was a place for Mermaids and that I would know just where.

Well, where DO the Mermaids stand? All the "Mermaids"—all those who are different, who do not fit the norm and who do not accept the available boxes and pigeonholes?

Answer that question and you can build a school, a nation, or a world on it.

And what was my answer at the moment? Well, every once in a while I say the right thing. "The Mermaid stands right here by the King of the Sea!" says I.

It is not true, by the way, that mermaids do not exist. I know at least one personally. I have held her hand.

Chapter 3
The Good Stuff

The cardboard box is marked "The Good Stuff." As I write, I can see the box where it is stored on a high shelf in my studio. I like being able to see it when I look up. The box contains those odds and ends of personal treasures that have survived many bouts of clean-it-out-and-throw-it-away that seize me from time to time. The box has passed through the screening done as I've moved from house to house and hauled stuff from attic to attic. A thief looking into the box would not take anything—he couldn't get a dime for any of it. But if the house ever catches on fire, the box goes with me when I run.

One of the keepsakes in the box is a small paper bag. Lunch size. Though the top of the bag is sealed with duct tape, staples, and several paper clips, there is a ragged rip in one side through which the contents may be seen.

This particular lunch sack has been in my care for maybe fourteen years now. But it really belongs to my daughter, Molly. Soon after she came of school age, she became an enthusiastic participant in packing the morning lunches for herself, her brothers, and me. Each bag got a share of sandwiches, apples, milk money, and sometimes a note or a treat. One morning Molly handed me two bags as I was about to leave. One was a regular lunch sack. And then there was the one with the duct tape and the staples and the paper clips. "Why two bags?" "The other one is something else." "What's in it?" "Ah, just some stuff—take it with you." So not wanting to hold court over the matter, I stuffed both sacks into my briefcase, kissed the child, and rushed off.

At midday, while hurriedly scarfing down my real lunch, I tore open Molly's bag and shook out the contents. Two hair ribbons, three small stones, a plastic dinosaur, a pencil stub, a tiny seashell, two animal crackers, a marble, a used lipstick, a small doll, two chocolate kisses, and thirteen pennies.

I smiled. How charming. Rising to hustle off to all the important business of the afternoon, I swept the desk clean—into the wastebasket—leftover lunch, Molly's junk, and all. There wasn't anything in there I needed.

That evening Molly came to stand beside me while I was reading the paper. "Where's my bag?" "What bag?" "You know, the one I gave you this morning." "I left it at the office, why?" "I forgot to put this note in it." She hands over the note. "Besides, I want it back." "Why?" "Those are my things in the sack, Daddy, the ones I really like—I thought you might like to play with them, but now I want them back. You didn't lose the bag, did you, Daddy?" Tears puddled in her eyes. "Oh no, I just forgot to bring it home, " I lied. "Bring it home tomorow, okay?" "Sure thing—don't worry." As she hugged my neck with relief, I unfolded the note that had not got into the sack: "I love you, Daddy."

Oh.

And also—uh-oh.

I looked long at the face of my child.

She was right—what was in that sack was indeed "something else."

Molly had given me her treasures. All that a seven-year-old held dear. Love in a paper sack. And I had missed it. Not only missed it but had thrown it in the wastebasket because "there wasn't anything in there I needed." Oh, dear God.

It wasn't the first time or the last time I felt my Daddy Permit was about to run out.

It was a long trip back to the office. But there was nothing else to be done. So I went. The pilgrimage of a penitent. Just ahead of the janitor, I picked up the wastebasket and poured the contents out on my desk. I was sorting it all out when the janitor came in to do his chores. "Lose something?" he asked. "Yeah, my mind." "It's probably in there, all right. What's it look like and I'll help you find it?" I started not to tell him. But I couldn't feel any more a fool then than I was already in fact, so I told him. He didn't laugh. He smiled. "I got kids, too." So the brotherhood of fools searched the trash and found the jewels and he smiled at me and I smiled at him. You are never alone in these things. Never.

After washing the mustard off the dinosaurs and spraying the whole thing with breath-freshener to kill the smell of onions, I carefully smoothed out the wadded ball of brown paper into a semifunctional bag and put the treasures inside and carried the whole thing home gingerly, like an injured kitten And the next evening I returned it to Molly, no questions asked, no explanations offered. The bag didn't look so good, but the stuff was all there and that's what counted. After dinner I asked her to tell me about the stuff in the sack, and so she took it all out one piece at a time and placed the objects in a row on the dining room table.

It took a long time to tell. Everything had a story, a memory, or was attached to dreams and imaginary friends. Fairies had brought some of the things. And I had given her the chocolate kisses, and she had kept them for when she needed them. I managed to say, "I see" very wisely several times in the telling. And as a matter of fact, I did see.

To my suprise, Molly gave the bag to me once again several days later. Same ratty bag. Same stuff inside. I felt forgiven. And trusted. And loved. And a little more comfortable wearing the title of Father. Over several months the bag went with me from time to time. It was never clear to me why I did or did not get it on a given day. I began to think of it as the Daddy Prize, and I tried to be good the night before so I might be given it the next morning.

In time Molly turned her attention to other things . . . found other treasures . . . lost interest in the game . . . grew up. Something. Me? I was left holding the bag. She gave it to me one morning and never asked for its return. And so I have it still.

Sometimes I think of all the times in this sweet life when I must have missed the affection I was being given. A friend calls this "standing knee-deep in the river and dying of thirst."

So the worn paper sack is there in the box on the shelf left over from a time when a child said, "Here—this is the best I've got. Take it—it's yours. Such as I have, give I thee."

I missed it the first time But it's my bag now.

Chapter 4

Rites of Passage

In most American high schools there is someone who teaches driver training. It's a job that anybody with half a brain could do—and anybody who wants the job doesn't have much ambition or talent or skill. Maybe.

Nevertheless, I would like to teach driver training for a while. It would be an honor, now that I see it the way Old Mr. Perry sees it. The students call him that. "Old Mr. Perry." They also call him "the Driving Master" and "Obi Wan Kenobi." Since the latter name refers to the Wise One in the Star Wars trilogy, I asked some students the reason, and they said: Take a ride and see. And so I did.

—So you're the man who teaches Driving Training?

—Well, that's my job title, yes.

—I'd like to know what you really DO. The students say you are one of the really fine people around school—a "truly maximum dude," to quote one.

—You really want to know?

—I really want to know.

—Guess this sounds presumptuous, but I think of myself as a shaman—one who is involved in helping young men and women move through a rite of passage—and my job is getting them to think about this time in their lives.

Most of them are almost sixteen. They know a lot more about life and sex and alcohol and drugs and money than their parents or their teachers give them credit for. And they are physically pretty much what they're going to be.

But we don't have any cultural rituals to acknowledge this. There's no ceremony, changing of clothes, or roles or public statement that says, This isn't a kid anymore—this is a young adult.

The only thing we do is give them a driver's license. Learning to drive a car means you move out of the backseat and into the driver's seat. You aren't a passenger anymore. Now you're in charge. You can go where you want to go. You have power now. So that's what we talk about. That power.

—But what about actually learning to operate a vehicle?

—Oh, that comes easily enough—some driving time with suggestions—reading the manual —see they *want* it all enough to work at it on their own. I don't talk much about that–they have to pass a test, and it usually takes care of itself.

—So what do you talk about when you're out driving?

—Talk about that power—opportunity—responsibility. About dreams, hopes, fears—about "someday" and "what if." I listen a lot, mostly. I'm not a parent, a schoolteacher or a neighbor, and they hardly ever see me except when it's just the two of us out in a car cruising around. So I'm safe to talk to. They tell me about love and money and plans, and they ask me what it was like when I was their age, and what I wish I knew back then that I know now.

—Will you take me out for a ride? My driving could be improved.

And so we went. And so it was. My driving was improved–along with my sense of place and purpose.

This experience with the Driving Master emphasizes the profound truth of a story that's been around a long time. If you don't know the story, it's time you heard it. And if you know it, you ought to hear it again once in a while.

The story says that a traveler from Italy came to the French town of Chartres to see the great church that was being built there. Arriving at the end of the day, he went to the site just as the workmen were leaving for home. He asked one man, covered with dust, what he did there. The man replied that he was a stonemason. He spent his days carving rocks. Another man, when asked, said he was a glassblower who spent his days making slabs of colored glass. And still another workman replied that he was a blacksmith who pounded iron for a living.

Wandering into the unfinished edifice, the traveler came upon an older woman, armed with a broom, sweeping up the stone chips and wood shavings and glass shards from the day's work. "What are you doing?" he asked.

The woman paused, leaning on her broom, and looked up toward the high arches, replied, "Me?" I'm building a cathedral for the Glory of Almighty God."

I've often thought about the people of Chartres. They began something they knew they would never see completed. They built for something larger than themselves. They had a magnificent vision.

And for Jack Perry, it is the same. He will never see his students grow up. Few teachers do. But from where he is and with what he has, he serves a vision of how the world ought to be.

That old woman of Chartres was a spiritual ancestor of the man who teaches driver training, who is building a cathedral to the human enterprise in his own quiet way. From him the kids learn both to drive a car and drive a life—with care.

Chapter 5
Personal Perception

The teacher is quiet. He is thinking. I can't believe I am doing this. He pulls on rubber gloves, reaches into a white plastic bag, and pulls out a human brain. A real no-kidding human brain.

The students in the room are very quiet. They are thinking, I can't believe he is really doing this.

The students are also thinking, If he hands it to me I will DIE, JUST DIE!

And sure enough, he hands it to them. They do not die.

When the brain comes back to him, the teacher tosses it across the table to the rubber-gloved quarterback of the football team, and he tosses it to his rubber-gloved tight end. And there was laughter as the tight end drops the brain on the table and the brain bounces.

To explain: In this beginning drawing class, I had been lecturing about the impact of brain research on the process of art, and we'd use pictures and diagrams and anatomy charts. We'd even tossed around a cantaloupe to get the feel of the size of a brain, but somehow brains remained a bit abstract. The students had that expression on their faces that meant this is getting b-o-r-i-n-g.

A freshman girl says, "I can bring a human brain to school if you want—my father has lots of them."

Well, it turns out that her daddy is a bona fide research neurosurgeon at the medical school and has jars and jars of brains in his lab and he would be pleased to have us see the real thing. So, sure, I can handle this. "Bring a brain to school!" I shout at the departing class. "All of you!!"

Sure enough, a week later, the freshman girl shows up with a brain in a bag.

"Well, Mr. Fulghum, what do you think?"

This is what the students call an "oooo-wow" moment of monumental proportion.

"I have one of these things between my ears," I said. It is made up entirely of raw meat at the moment. It is fueled by yesterday's baloney sandwich, potato chips, and chocolate milk. And everything I am doing at the moment—everything I have ever done or will do—passes through this lump. I made it; I own it. And it is the most mysterious thing on earth.

"Now I can kind of understand the mechanical work of the brain—stimulating breathing, moving blood, directing protein traffic. It's all chemistry and electricity. It's a motor and, I know about motors.

"But this three-pound raw-meat motor also contains a recipe for how to cook a turkey, the remembered smell of my junior-high locker room, all my sorrows, the face of my wife when she was young, the sound of the first cry of my firstborn son, the words to the fight song of St. Olaf' College, fifty years' worth of dreams, how to tie my shoelaces. There's an image of Van Gogh's "Sunflowers." And it's all there in the MEAT.

"One cubic centimeter of the brain contains ten billion bits of information and it processes five thousand bits a second. And somehow it evolved over a zillion years from a molten ball of rock. Earth, which will itself fall into the sun someday and be no more. Why? How?

"*That's* what I think."

"Oooo-wow," chorus the students.

Once again the brain is passed around from hand to hand, slowly, solemnly. Once again it is very quiet. The Mystery of Mysteries is present, and it includes us.

The single most powerful statement to come out of brain research in the last twenty-five years is this: *We are as different from one another on the inside of our heads as we appear to be different from one another on the outside of our heads.*

Look around and see the infinite variety of human heads—skin, hair, age, ethnic characteristics, size, color, shape. And know that on the inside such differences are even greater—what we know, how we learn, how we process information, what we remember and forget, our strategies for functioning and coping. Add to that the understanding that the "world" out "there" is as much a *projection* from inside our heads as it is a *perception*, and pretty soon you are up against the realization that it is a miracle that we communicate at all. It is almost unbelievable that we are dealing with the same reality.

From a practical point of view, day by day, this kind of information makes me a little more patient with the people I live with. I am less inclined to protest, "Why don't you see it the way I do?" and more inclined to say, "You see it *that* way? Holy cow! How amazing!"

This set me to thinking about Einstein's brain, which as I understand, is somewhere in Missouri in a lab in a jar now. And his brain was removed and studied to see if it was special in some way. (*No, it wasn't. It wasn't his equipment, but what he did with it, that cracked the window on the Mystery of Mysteries.*) When old Big Al was in residence at the Institute for Advanced Studies at Princeton, a guest once asked to be shown Einstein's laboratory. And the great man smiled, held up his fountain pen, pointed at his head. (*Oooo-wow*).

Chapter 6
Light Reflections

"Are there any questions?" That's an offer that comes at the end of college lectures and long meetings. Said when an audience is not only overdosed with information, but when there is no time left anyhow.

But if there is a little time left, I usually ask the most important question of all: "What is the meaning of life?"

Once, and only once, I asked that question and got a serious answer. One that is with me still.

First, I must tell you where this happened, because the place has a power of its own. Near the village of Gonia on a rocky bay on the island of Crete, sits a Greek Orthodox monastery. Alongside it, on land donated by the monastery, is an institute dedicated to human understanding and peace, and especially to rapprochement between Germans and Cretans. An improbable task, given the bitter residue of wartime.

This site is very important, because it overlooks the small airstrip of Maleme where Nazi paratroopers invaded Crete and were attacked by peasants wielding kitchen knives and hay scythes. The retribution was terrible. The populations of whole villages were lined up and shot for assaulting Hitler's finest troops. High above the institute is a cemetery with a single cross marking the mass grave of Cretan partisans. And across the bay on yet another hill is the burial ground of the Nazi paratroopers. The memorials are so placed that all might see and never forget. Hate was the only weapon the Cretans had at the end, and it was a weapon many vowed never to give up. Never ever.

Against this heavy curtain of history, the existence of an institute devoted to healing the wounds of war is a fragile paradox. How has it come to be here? The answer is a simple: A man. Christos Papaderos.

A doctor of philosophy, a teacher, politician, resident of Athens but a son of this soil. At war's end he came to believe that the Germans and the Cretans had much to give one another—much to learn from one another. That they had an example to set. For if they could forgive each other and construct a creative relationship, then any people could.

To make a lovely story short, Papaderos succeeded. The institute became a reality, and it was in fact a source of productive interaction between the two countries. Books have been written on the dreams that were realized by what people gave to people here at the institute.

By the time I came to the institute for a summer session, Christos Papaderos had become a living legend. One look at him and you saw his strength and intensity—his energy, physical power, courage, intelligence, passion, and vivacity radiated from his person. And to speak to him, to shake his hand, to be in a room with him when he spoke, was to experience his extraordinary electric humanity. Few men live up to their reputations when you get close. Christos Papaderos was an exception.

At the last session on the last morning of a two-week seminar on Greek culture, led by intellectuals and experts in their fields who were recruited by Papaderos from across Greece, Papaderos rose from his chair at the back of the room, walked to the front, where he stood in the bright Greek sunlight of an open window and looked out.

He turned. "Are there any questions?"

Quiet quilted the room. These two weeks had generated enough questions for a lifetime, but for now there was only silence.

"No questions?" Papaderos swept the room with his eyes.

So. I asked.

"Dr. Papaderos, what is the meaning of life?"

The usual laughter followed, people stirred to go, but Papaderos held up his hand and stilled the room and looked at me for a long time, asking with his eyes if I was serious and seeing from my eyes that yes, I was.

"I will answer that question."

Taking his wallet out of his hip pocket, he fished into a leather fold and brought out a very small round mirror, about the size of a quarter.

And what he said went like this:

"When I was a child, during the war, we were very poor and we lived in a remote village. One day, on the road, I found the broken pieces of a mirror. A German motorcycle had been wrecked in that place.

"I tried to find all the pieces and put them together, but it was not possible, so I kept only the largest piece. This one. And by scratching it on a stone I made it round. I began to play with it as a toy—became fascinated by the fact that I could reflect light into dark places where the sun would never shine—into deep holes and dark closets. It became a game for me to get light into the most inaccessible places I could find.

"I kept the little mirror, and as I went about my growing up, I would take it out in idle moments and continue the challenge of the game. As I became a man, I grew to understand that this was not just a child's game but a metaphor for what I might do with my life. I came to understand that I am not the light or the source of light. But light—truth, understanding, knowledge —is there, and it will only shine in many dark places if I reflect it.

"I am a fragment of a mirror whose whole design and shape I do not know. Nevertheless, with what I have I can reflect light into the dark places of this world—into the black places in the hearts of men—and change some things in some people. Perhaps others may see and do likewise. This is what I am about. This is the meaning of my life."

And then he took his small mirror and, holding it very carefully, caught the bright rays of daylight streaming through the window and reflected them onto my face and onto my hands folded there on the desk.

Much of what I experienced in the way of information about Greek culture and history that summer is long gone from my memory. But in the wallet of my mind I carry a small round mirror still.

Are there any questions?

Chapter 7
The Stick-Polishing Fantasy

The man next door cleaned his gutters yesterday—downspouts too. He's done it before. I saw him last year. Amazing. I was forty years old before I even knew that people cleaned gutters and downspouts. And I haven't been able to get around to doing it once yet.

I live in awe of people who get those jobs done. The people who live orderly lives. The ones who always do what needs to be done and do it right.

These people also have filing cabinets with neat, up-to-date, relevant files And they can find things around the house when they need them. There is order under their sinks, in their closets, and in the trunks of their cars.

Yes, there *are* such people. I see them every day all around me.

Well. I'm not one of them. Out of the frying pan, into the spilt milk is more me. Most of the time daily life is a lot like an endless chore of chasing chickens in a large pen. Never mind the details.

But I have a recurring fantasy that sees me through. It is my stick-polishing fantasy. One day a committee of elders will come to my door and tell me it is time to perform the ritual of the polished stick—a rite of passage for the good-at-heart-but-chronically-disorganized.

Here's the way it works. You get selected for this deal because you are such a good person at heart, and it is time you were let off the hook. First, a week of your life is given to you free of all obligations. And your calendar is wiped clean. No committee meetings, no overdue anything—bills, correspondence, or unanswered telephone calls. You are taken to a nice place, where it is all quiet and serene and Zen. You are cared for. Fed well. And often affirmed. And your task is simply this: to spend a week polishing a stick. They give you some sandpaper and lemon oil and rags. And, of course, the stick—a nice but ordinary piece of wood. And all you have to do is polish it. As well as you can. Whenever you feel like it. That's it: *polish the stick.*

At the end of the week the elders will return and they will examine your work. They will praise you for your expertise, your sensitivity, and your spiritual insight. "No stick was ever polished quite like *this*!" they will exclaim. Your picture will appear on TV and in the papers. You will be escorted home in quiet triumph.

Your family and neighbors will give you looks of respect. And as you pass in the streets, people will smile knowingly and wave and give you the thumbs-up sign.

But more than that. From this time forward, you may ignore your gutters and downspouts. Your checkbooks and files and forms and closets and drawers and taxes and even the trunk of your car will be taken care of for you. You are now exempt from those concerns. You are forever released from the bond of Things to Do. For you have *polished the stick*! Be proud, stick polisher! This is really something. And, it is enough.

Oh, don't I wish.

Chapter 8
Fathers and Sons

This is a story about a father and a son and it begins in 1963.

From deep in the canyoned aisles of a supermarket comes what sounds like a small-scale bus wreck followed by an air raid. If you followed the running box-boy with mop and broom, you would come upon a young father, his three-year-old son, an upturned shopping cart, and a good part of the pickles shelf—all in a heap on the floor.

The father is calm because he is thinking about running away from home. Now. Just walking away, getting into the car, driving away somewhere down South, changing his name, getting a job as a paperboy or a cook in an all-night diner. Something—anything—that doesn't involve contact with three-year-olds.

Oh sure, someday he may find all this amusing, but in the most private part of his heart he is sorry he has children, sorry he married, sorry he grew up, and, above all, sorry that this particular son cannot be traded in for a model that works He will not and cannot say these things to anybody, ever, but they are there and they are not funny.

Later, the father sits in his car in the parking lot holding the sobbing child in his arms until the child sleeps. He drives home, carries the child up to his crib and tucks him in. The father looks at the sleeping child for a long time. And the father does not run away from home.

Now we are 15 years later in this story. It is 1978.

The same man paces my living room, carelessly cursing and weeping by turns. In his hand is what's left of a letter which has been crumpled into a ball and then uncrumpled again several times. The letter is from his eighteen-year-old son (*the same son*). The pride of his father's eye—or was until today's mail.

The son says he hates him and never wants to see him again. The son is going to run away from home. Because of his terrible father. The son thinks the father is a failure as a parent. The son thinks the father is a jerk.

What the father thinks of the son right now is somewhat incoherent, but it isn't nice.

He really is a good man and a fine father. The evidence of that is overwhelming. And the son is quality goods as well. Just like his father, they say.

"Why did this happen to me?" the father shouts at the ceiling.

Well, he had a son. That's all it takes. And it doesn't do any good to explain about that right now. First you have to live through it.

The story is now.

The story is always. It's been lived thousands of times, over thousands of years, and literature is full of examples of tragic endings, to the story, including that of Oedipus. The sons leave, kick away, burn all the bridges, never to be seen again. But sometimes they come back in their own way and in their own time and take their own fathers in their arms. That ending is an old one, too. The father of the Prodigal Son could tell you.

The story picks up again in 1988.

Same man, same son. The son is twenty-eight now, married, with his own three-year-old son, home, career, all the rest. And the father is fifty.

Three mornings a week I see them out jogging together around 6:00 A.M. As they cross a busy street, I see the son look both ways, with a hand on his father's elbow to hold him back from the danger of oncoming cars, protecting him from harm. I hear them laughing as they run on up the hill into the morning. And when they sprint toward home, the son doesn't run ahead, he runs alongside his father at his pace.

They love each other a lot. You can see it.

And they are very careful of each other—they have been through a lot together, but it's all right now.

One of their favorite stories is about once upon a time in a supermarket . . .

Chapter 9
Donnie and the Leaves

The rap on the door was sharp, urgent, insistent—rappity–rappity–rappity *rap* . . . Me, rushing to the door, preparing for an emergency. A small boy. Odd expression. Hands me a scrawled note on a much-folded paper: "My name is Donnie. I will rake your leaves. $1 a yard. I am deaf. You can write to me. I can read. I rake good."

Like a pilot in a fog relying on limited instruments, the boy looks intently at my face for information. He knows I have leaves for he has seen them. And mine is the *only* yard in the neighborhood with leaves, in fact. He knows his price is right. And so solemnly he holds out pencil and paper for my reply. How can I explain to him the importance of the scientific experiment going on in my backyard?

"My name is Donnie. I will rake your leaves. $1 a yard. I am deaf. You can write to me. I can read. I rake good." And he holds out the pencil and paper with patience and hope and goodwill.

What would I do if he wasn't deaf? What will it do for him if I say no? If I say yes? What difference? We stand in each other's long silence, inarticulate for different reasons. In the same motion that he turns to go, I reach for the pencil and paper to write, solemnly: "Yes. Yes, I would like to have my leaves raked." A grave nod from the attentive businessmanchild. "Do you do it when they are wet?"

"Yes," he writes.

"Do you have your own rake?"

"No."

"This is a big yard—there are lots of leaves."

"Yes."

"I think I should give you two dollars."

A smile. "Three," he writes.

A grin.

And we have a contract. The rake is produced, and Donnie the deaf leaf-raker goes to work in the fast-falling November twilight. In silence he rakes. In silence I watch—through the window of the dark house. Are there any sounds at all in his mind? I wonder. Or only the hollow, empty sea-sound I get when I put my fingers in my ears as tightly as I can.

Carefully he rakes the leaves into a large pile, as instructed. Carefully he goes back over the yard picking up missed leaves by hand and carrying them to the pile.

Signing that he must go because it is dark and he must go home to eat, he leaves the work unfinished. Having paid in advance, I wonder if he will return. At age forty-five, I am cynical. Too cynical. Come morning, he has returned to his task, first checking the previously raked yard for latecomers. He takes pride in his work. The yard is leaf-free. I note his picking up several of the brightest yellow leaves and putting them into the pocket of his sweat shirt. Along with a whole handful of helicoptered seeds.

Rappity-rappity-rappity-rap! He reports to the door, signing that the work is done. As he goes off up the street I see him tossing one seed into the air at a time.

Tomorrow I will go out and push the pile of leaves into the compost heap at the bottom of the ravine behind our house. I will do it in silence. The leaves let go, the seeds let go, and I must let go sometimes, too.

Hold on, Donnie, hold on.

Chapter 10

Larry Walters and His Flying Dream Machine

Now let me tell you about Larry Walters, my hero. Walters is a truck driver, thirty-three years old. He is sitting in his lawn chair in his backyard, wishing he could fly. For as long as he could remember, he wanted to go *up*. To be able to just rise right up in the air and see for a long way. But the time, and the money, and the education, and the opportunity to be a pilot were not his. And hang gliding was too dangerous, and any good place for gliding was too far away. Anyhow, so he spent a lot of summer afternoons sitting in his backyard in his ordinary old aluminum lawn chair—the kind with the webbing and the rivets. Just like the one you've got in your backyard.

The next chapter in this story is carried by the newspapers and television. There's old Larry Walters up in the air over Los Angeles. Flying at last. Really getting UP there. Still sitting in his aluminum lawn chair, but it's hooked on to forty five helium-filled surplus weather ballons. Larry has a parachute on, a CB radio in his lap, a six-pack of beer, some peanut butter and jelly sandwiches, and a BB gun to pop some of the balloons to come down. And instead of just being a couple of hundred feet over his own neighborhood, he shot up eleven thousand feet, right through the approach corridor to the L. A. International Airport.

Walters is a taciturn man. When asked by the press why he did it, he said: "You can't just sit there forever." When asked if he was scared, he answered: "Wonderfully so." When asked if he would do it again, he said: "Nope." And asked if he was glad that he did it, he grinned from ear to ear and said: "Oh, yes."

The human race sits in its chair. On the one hand is the message that says there's nothing left to do. And the Larry Walterses of the earth are busy tying balloons to their chairs, directed by dreams and imagination to do their thing.

The human race sits in its chair. On the one hand is the message that the human situation is hopeless. And the Larry Walterses of the earth soar upward knowing anything is possible, and sending back the message from eleven thousand feet: "I've done it, I really done it. I'm FLYING!"

It's the spirit here that counts. The time may be long, the vehicle may be strange or unexpected. But if the dream is held close to the heart, and imagination is applied to what there is close at hand, everything is still possible.

But wait! Some cynic from the edge of the crowd insists that human beings still *can't really* fly. Not like birds, anyway. True. But somewhere in some little garage, some maniac with a gleam in his eye is scarfing vitamins and mineral supplements, and practicing flapping his arms faster and faster and faster and who knows . . .